EMILY BRONTË

Women Writers

General Editors: *Eva Figes* and *Adele King*

Published titles:
Margaret Atwood, Barbara Hill Rigney
Anne Brontë, Elizabeth Langland
Charlotte Brontë, Pauline Nestor
Emily Brontë, Lyn Pykett
Fanny Burney, Judy Simons
Willa Cather, Susie Thomas
Sylvia Plath, Susan Bassnett
Christina Stead, Diana Brydon
Eudora Welty, Louise Westling
Women in Romanticism, Meena Alexander

Forthcoming:
Jane Austen, Meenakshi Mukherjee
Elizabeth Barrett Browning, Marjorie Stone
Elizabeth Bowen, Phyllis Lassner
Ivy Compton Burnett, Kathy Gentile
Colette, Diana Holmes
Emily Dickinson, Joan Kirkby
George Eliot, Kristin Brady
Mrs Gaskell, Jane Spencer
Doris Lessing, Barbara Hill Rigney
Katherine Mansfield, Diane DeBell
Christina Rossetti, Linda Marshall
Jean Rhys, Carol Rumens
Stevie Smith, Catherine Civello
Muriel Spark, Judith Sproxton
Edith Wharton, Katherine Joslin
Virginia Woolf, Clare Hanson

Women Writers

Emily Brontë

Lyn Pykett

BARNES & NOBLE BOOKS
Savage, Maryland

© Lyn Pykett 1989

First published in the USA 1989 by
BARNES & NOBLE BOOKS
8705 Bollman Place
Savage, Maryland 20763

Printed in Hong Kong

ISBN: 0–389–20880–9 Cloth
      0–333–20881–7 Paper

Library of Congress Cataloging in Publication Data
Pykett, Lyn.
   Emily Brontë / Lyn Pykett.
      p.   cm. — (Women writers)
   Bibliography: p.
   Includes index.
   ISBN 0–389–20880–9. — ISBN 0–389–20881–7 (pbk.)
   1. Brontë, Emily, 1818–1848—Criticism and interpretation.
2. Women and literature—England—History—19th century.   I. Title.
II. Series.
PR4173.P94   1989
823'.8—dc20
                                                     89–34595
                                                         CIP

Contents

Acknowledgements

I would like to thank members of the Northern Network group who helped me to clarify some of the ideas in Chapter 5. Particular thanks to the women members of the English Department of the University of Leeds for their hospitality on this occasion. Thanks are also due to staff and students of the English Departments at Aberystwyth and Swansea, who probably got more of Emily Brontë's poetry than they had expected at a colloquium on nineteenth-century women writers at Gregynog. My greatest debt is to my husband, who neither ironed my shirts, nor typed up the fruits of my labours, but who took on much more than his fair share of childcare, and left me to my own (de)vices.

Editors' Preface

The study of women's writing has been long neglected by a male critical establishment both in academic circles and beyond. As a result, many women writers have either been unfairly neglected, or have been marginalised in some way, so that their true influence and importance has been ignored. Other women writers have been accepted by male critics and academics, but on terms which seem, to many women readers of this generation, to be false or simplistic. In the past the internal conflicts involved in being a woman in a male-dominated society have been largely ignored by readers of both sexes, and this has affected our reading of women's work. The time has come for a serious re-assessment of women's writing in the light of what we understand today

This series is designed to help in that re-assessment. All the books are written by women, because we believe that men's understanding of feminist critique is only, at best, partial. And besides, men have held the floor quite long enough.

Eva Figes
Adele King

1 Emily Brontë: A Life Hidden From History

The life of Emily Brontë is shrouded in mystery, and she remains an elusive and mysterious figure, despite the efforts of her latest and most scrupulous biographer, Edward Chitham,[1] to unravel the myths and legends that have surrounded her life and work. At the heart of the problem is the personality of the subject of our attention and speculations, the reserved and private figure of Emily Brontë herself. As John Hewish has noted, 'This author's life and personality are monolithic and tend to be biographer-proof'.[2]

The biographer's problem is compounded, on the one hand, by the 'initial lack of material on which to base a biography' (WG, vii) and, on the other hand, by the nature of the material that we have. The basic material usually considered necessary for a fully historical understanding of an author's life and work – letters, diaries, journals, notebooks, working manuscripts, reported conversations etc. – are notably lacking in the case of Emily Brontë. This self-confessedly poor correspondent wrote few letters, of which only three have survived. It would appear that she did not keep a diary or journal, and the only autobiographical records that remain are the fragments of a diary she wrote with her sister Anne in November 1834 and June 1837, and two 'Birthday Papers', again written with her close collaborator Anne, dated 30 July 1841 and 30 July 1845.

On the other hand, the evidence that we do have presents its own problems. Emily Brontë's life story comes to us, like the life stories of her own fictional creations in

1

Wuthering Heights, refracted through the lives and stories of others: through the hazy recollections of neighbouring villagers; the scattered reminiscences of those who were more directly acquainted with her more sociable and more successful sister Charlotte; and through Elizabeth Gaskell's *Life of Charlotte Brontë*. In each case Emily remains elusive, a figure glimpsed in the margins of her sister's life, re-seen and reinterpreted by those seeking to discover in their reserved acquaintance the sort of woman who could have been the author of the powerfully disturbing *Wuthering Heights*. Most importantly, perhaps, Emily Brontë has been delivered to literary history through the refracting lens of her sister Charlotte. In the Biographical Notice and Editor's Preface which she provided for the second edition of *Wuthering Heights* Charlotte sought to interpret and domesticate the phenomenon of that novel for an unsympathetic and potentially hostile Victorian audience, by constructing a portrait of the female genius that would not seriously disrupt the prevailing ideal of the feminine.

These biographical problems are, perhaps, the inevitable consequence of the fact that, in some senses, the most extraordinary aspect of Emily Brontë's life was her authorship of the poems and novel for which she is admired. We are all, no doubt, familiar with the legendary tales of the isolated parsonage at Haworth, and the brooding precocious genius, repressed spinsterhood or turbulent drunkenness of its inmates. However, although Emily Brontë's life story has often been presented in terms of the plot of a Gothic novel, in many ways the life of the atypical and extraordinary woman whom literary history has discovered in the author of *Wuthering Heights*, could be seen as a typical nineteenth-century woman's life: private, domestic, hidden from history. In this contrast, between Emily Brontë the extraordinary woman, the Romantic genius, the writer, and Emily Brontë the self-contained and, on the whole, dutiful daughter of the parsonage we have the central riddle and the central conflict of this woman's life.

The essential details of Emily Brontë's outwardly uneventful life are soon given. Emily Jane Brontë was born on 30 July 1818, the fifth of a family of six children. On 20 April 1820 the Reverend Patrick Brontë and his family moved from the parsonage at Thornton, in the parish of Bradford, to that of Haworth where Emily, apart from a few brief and troubled absences, was to spend the remainder of her relatively short life. Before her own death on 19 December 1848 Emily suffered the loss of her mother and two of her sisters, and had to witness the moral and physical decline of a brother who was destroyed by a hopeless sexual infatuation, by equally deluded fantasies of literary success, and by drugs and alcohol.

Like many children in the nineteenth century Emily Brontë and her siblings were early acquainted with physical suffering and death. Emily's earliest years were lived out in the shadow of a mother weakened by frequent pregnancies who finally succumbed to cancer at the age of thirty eight in September 1821. Emily Brontë thus became one of those motherless daughters who figure so prominently in Victorian fiction. Indeed, as numerous commentators have observed, a significantly high proportion of nineteenth-century women writers seem to have lost their mothers in early childhood, a situation which perhaps fostered independence, self-definition, and creativity, by removing at least one of 'the constraints to female conformity which a mother so frequently imposes'.[3] Their mother's exile to the sick room and her early death, their father's concern for his wife, his duties in the parish, and his retreat to his study, forced the Brontë children to rely on their own resources, and led to that close bonding and mutual interdependence which has been noted by most observers of the family. The self-enclosed, self-sufficiency of the sisters and their brother was reinforced by the arrival of Elizabeth Branwell, their mother's eldest sister, to take charge of her brother-in-law's house and children, and was to become more pronounced in later years as Charlotte recorded in her Biographical Notice.

> Resident in a remote district where education had made little progress, and where, consequently, there was no inducement to seek social intercourse beyond our own domestic circle, we were wholly dependent on ourselves and each other, on books and study for the enjoyments and occupations of life. (WH, 30)

On 25 November 1824 Emily Brontë followed the path taken by many motherless daughters of her class at this time and joined her three older sisters at the Clergy Daughters' School at Cowan Bridge near Kirkby Lonsdale, which was later to serve as Charlotte Brontë's model for Lowood School in *Jane Eyre*. After only six months, during which she had witnessed the effects of what is presumed to have been a typhoid epidemic at the school, and following the deaths from consumption of her sisters Maria and Elizabeth, Emily returned to Haworth with Charlotte. The first of her unhappy sojourns from home is recorded starkly in the school register, 'Emily Brontë 5³/₄ [she was in fact 6¹/₄.] 1824 Novbr 25th H Cough Reads very prettily & Works a little Left School June 1st 1825 Governess' (Chitham, *Life*, 36–7).

Emily remained at home until her second, again brief, foray into the world of boarding school in July 1835 when she joined Charlotte at Roe Head. In the meantime the pattern of her intensely private and domestic existence was established. Although she received little formal education during this ten year interval between schools Emily had access to a wide range of books, journals, and newspapers which, like her brother and sisters, she read avidly. *Blackwood's Magazine*, Sir Walter Scott's novels, poems and history, and the poems of Byron and of Shelley were Emily's particular favourites. Their eclectic reading fuelled the lively imaginations of the Brontë children and informed the plays and stories – all 'very strange ones' according to Charlotte – which they began to invent at this time, and which became an extremely important part of their lives. Charlotte and Branwell worked together on the chronicles of Angria, while Emily and Anne collaborated in the production of the saga of Gondal, a fictional island whose myths and legends were to preoccupy the two sisters throughout their lives.

Although the future author of *Wuthering Heights* may be glimpsed in the fabricator of the strange plays, most of the first-hand reports of this period tend to present Emily Brontë in the context of the domestic routine of the family, and suggest a life which was exceptional only in its extreme isolation. Charlotte's *The History of the Year (1829)*, for example, reveals Emily 'in the parlour, brushing the carpet',[4] while the fragment of a diary which Emily and Anne wrote in 1834 hardly suggests that the sixteen-year-old Emily is undergoing a stormy adolescence, and offers a sufficiently mundane impression of the daily life of the Haworth Parsonage.

This morning Branwell went down to Mr Driver's and brought news that Sir Robert Peel was going to be invited to stand for Leeds. Anne and I have been peeling apples for Charlotte to make an apple pudding . . . Taby said just now Come Anne pilloputate [i.e. pill a potato] . . . Papa opened the door and gave Branwell a letter saying Here Branwell read this and show it to your Aunt and Charlotte. The Gondals are discovering the interior of Gaaldine. Sally Mosley is washing in the back kitchin.

It is past twelve o'clock Anne and I have not tid[i]ed ourselves, done our bedwork or done our

lessons and we want to go out to play We are going
to have for dinner Boiled Beef, Turnips, potatoes and
apple pudding. The kitchin is in a very untidy state
Anne and I have not done our music exercise which
consists of *b major* Taby said on my putting a pen in her
face Ya pitter pottering there instead of pilling a potate.
I answered Dear, O Dear, O Dear I will derectly With
that I get up, take a knife and begin pilling. Finished
pilling the potatoes Papa going to walk Mr Sunderland
expected.

Anne and I say I wonder what we shall be and where
we shall be, if all goes on well in the year 1874. (LL I,
124–5)

Emily's tenuous grasp of spelling and punctuation adds
to the general impression of rather happy-go-lucky chaos
depicted in this scene of female industry. The passage
also neatly illustrates the separate masculine and feminine
spheres of Victorian family life. The sisters occupy a
private, domestic space, weaving their stories and fit-
ting in their lessons (or avoiding them) amidst shared
domestic chores, while father and son occupy themselves
with pursuits more suitable to their superior masculine
status, communicating with the world beyond the door-
step, participating in political discussion and bringing
news of the wider world to the women in the kitchen.

The sensuous warmth of the female domain of shared
domesticity which the diary fragment suggests, is precisely
what Charlotte yearned for on her second lone visit to
Brussels.

I should like uncommonly to be in the dining-room, or
in the back kitchen . . . cutting up the hash . . . and you
[Emily] standing by, watching that I put enough flour,
and not too much pepper . . . To complete the picture,

Tabby blowing the fire, in order to boil the potatoes to a sort of vegetable glue! (LL I, 305)

Each sister experiences the kitchen as a place of female companionship and shared employment, and also as a cocoon of domestic security. However, if Emily Brontë's autobiographical fragments portray the kitchen as the site of female self-definition, and domestic duty as the female vocation, these views are radically challenged by her activity as a writer and by the writings she produced. For Emily Brontë's life and works vividly demonstrate and explore the fact that cocoons can enmesh and stifle as well as shelter and nurture, and that there is nothing more secure than a prison. This tension between the cocoon and the prison, particularly in relation to the lives of women, underlies most of Emily Brontë's writings.

If it is difficult to discern the brooding, tormented genius of literary legend in the self-portrait of Emily's diary fragment, the tortured soul is almost equally difficult to discover in the picture of Emily provided by Charlotte's friend Ellen Nussey, whose recollections were documented after the legend had begun to develop. Ellen Nussey remembered the Emily she met on her first visit to Haworth in the summer of 1833 as a graceful, attractive girl with beautiful, if unflatteringly styled, hair and 'very beautiful eyes – kind, kindling, liquid eyes, but she did not often look at you; she was very reserved . . . she talked very little' (LL I, 112). It is only in an outdoor setting that Ellen Nussey's recollections suggest the author of the poems and the creator of *Wuthering Heights*:

In fine and suitable weather delightful rambles were made over the moors and down into the glens and ravines . . . Emily especially had a gleesome delight in these nooks of beauty, – her reserve for the time vanished.

It is, however, interesting to speculate to what extent Ellen Nussey's portrait of Emily is coloured by her reading of *Wuthering Heights*, particularly when she recalls how Emily,

> half reclining on a slab of stone played like a young child with the tadpoles in the water, making them swim about, and then fell to moralizing on the strong and the weak, the brave and the cowardly, as she chased them with her hand. (LL I, 113)

The extracts from Emily's diary fragment and Ellen Nussey's recollections indicate an enjoyment of daily domestic life, and of the surrounding countryside, which Emily Brontë was clearly reluctant to leave. This reluctance is demonstrated by the brevity of Emily's stay at Roe Head School, where Charlotte was already a teacher. Emily went to Roe Head in July 1835 but by November she had changed places with Anne and was back among her familiar surroundings. It is, perhaps, hardly surprising that the writer of that record of warm domestic anarchy that we noted earlier should have found the routine and discipline of a boarding school uncongenial. This certainly seems to have been Charlotte's view.

> Liberty was the breath of Emily's nostrils; without it she perished. The change from her own home to a school, and from her own very noiseless, very secluded, but unrestricted and inartificial mode of life, to one of disciplined routine . . . was what she failed in enduring . . . I felt in my heart she would die if she did not go home, and with this conviction obtained her recall. (quoted, WG, 55)

Emily's release from the 'disciplined routine' of school to the more liberal domestic routine of Haworth enabled her to resume writing in earnest. Most of her earliest surviving poems date from the period between her return from Roe Head and her departure, in September 1838, for a teaching post at Law Hill School near Halifax. Emily continued to work on her poems during her six months at Law Hill, where she may have gleaned some of the material that she was later to use in *Wuthering Heights*, and where she endured, in Charlotte's account, 'hard labour from six in the morning until near eleven at night, with only one half-hour of exercise between' (LL I, 162). Charlotte's fears that 'she will never stand it' were soon realised, and once more Emily returned to the domestic round and familiar scenes.

If the poems written in these years reveal conflict and inner turmoil, Emily's rare non-poetic utterances tell a different tale. The diary paper of June 1837 and the Birthday Papers which she wrote in July 1841 and 1845, in a joint venture with Anne, suggest industry and fortitude rather than angst. It is true that the first Birthday Paper displays anxiety about the future, but such concern is perfectly understandable in one of three unmarried sisters with an ailing aunt and father, and a feckless brother.

A scheme is at present in agitation for setting us up in a school of our own; . . . I hope and trust it may go on and prosper and answer our highest expectations. This day four years I wonder whether we shall still be dragging on in our present condition or established to our hearts' content. (LL, I, 238)

By the time of the second Birthday Paper in 1845 Emily is able to record with equanimity her nine month stay at the Hegers' school in Brussels, which, according to other commentators, she found arduous and unhappy, and where all her personal awkwardnesses seem to have been exacerbated.

> Our school scheme has been abandoned, and instead
> Charlotte and I went to Brussels on the 8th of February
> 1842 . . . C. and I returned from Brussels, November
> 8th, 1842, in consequence of aunt's death. (LL II, 49)

In fact 'aunt's death', and more particularly the legacies
she left to her nieces, removed many of Emily's practical
anxieties about the future.

> Now I don't desire a school at all, and none of us
> have any great longing for it. We have cash enough
> for our present wants, with a prospect of accumu-
> lation . . . I am quite contented for myself: not as idle
> as formerly . . . and having learnt to make the most of
> the present . . . seldom or never troubled with nothing
> to do, and merely desiring that everybody could be as
> comfortable as myself and as undesponding . . . I must
> hurry off now to my turning and ironing. (LL II, 51)

In the intervals of her turning and ironing, and baking
and cleaning, Emily took charge of the sisters' financial
affairs and invested their legacies in shares in the York
and Midland Railway Company.

In many ways it is difficult to reconcile Emily's self-image
in her Birthday Papers, and the capable practicality she
revealed in her management of her father's household and
her sisters' legacies, with Charlotte's version of her sister as a
woman entirely lacking in 'worldly wisdom', whose 'powers
were unadapted to the practical business of life' (WH, 35).
Nor is it entirely clear that Emily always failed (as Charlotte
contended) 'to defend her most manifest rights, [and] to
consult her most legitimate advantage'. Indeed Winifred
Gérin, quite plausibly, sees the course of events described in
the 1845 Birthday Paper as yet another example of Emily's
consistent ability to profit from any circumstances which
would keep her at home.

From the time of the 1845 Birthday Paper, until Emily's death in 1848, the three Brontë sisters remained at home. Domestic life at this time could have been neither quiet nor happy, owing to Branwell's rapid decline into debt and drunkenness following his dismissal from his tutorship at Thorp Green and his subsequent rejection by his newly widowed former employer, Mrs Robinson. However, despite Branwell, this was a period of intense literary activity for all three sisters, in which Charlotte (according to her own account in the Biographical Notice) took the lead in fanning the flames of her sisters' ambitions and encouraging them to seek the publication of their poems. It was Charlotte too who stage-managed the attempts to publish the 'prose tales' which were also produced during this flurry of literary activity, in which 'the mere effort to succeed had given a wonderful zest to existence' (WH, 32).

Much of our knowledge about this period of writing and preparing works for publication comes from Charlotte's Biographical Notice. Indeed, since 1850 when this Notice and the Preface to the new edition of *Wuthering Heights* appeared, Charlotte Brontë has served as that interpreter whom she considered 'ought always to have stood between Emily and the world' (WH, 36). It is time to look more closely at Charlotte's role as her sister's interpreter, and to uncover some of the assumptions about women, and particularly women writers, which underlie the version of Emily Brontë which Charlotte Brontë has delivered to literary history.

In her Biographical Notice and the Editor's Preface to the 1850 edition of *Wuthering Heights* Charlotte Brontë engages in the double activity of attempting to understand and come to terms with her sister's poems and novel, and of translating both the writer and her writings to the world at large. She does this mainly by having recourse to a theory of genius and a Romantic theory of creativity in which the literary work comes unbidden to the possessor of the creative gift.

> [T]he writer who possesses the creative gift owns
> something of which he is not always master . . . He may
> lay down rules and devise principles, and to rules and
> principles it will perhaps for years lie in subjection; and
> then, haply without any warning of revolt, there comes a
> time when it will no longer consent to 'harrow the vallies,
> or be bound with a band in the furrow' . . . [and] you
> have little choice left but quiescent adoption. (WH, 40)

Emily, we are told, was the possessor of such gifts,
and 'wrote from the impulse of nature, the dictates of
intuition', and thus could not be held directly responsible
for what she had written – 'Having formed these beings,
she did not know what she had done' (WH, 39). Charlotte
attempts to detach her sister from her wild impassioned
works by presenting her as an exaggerated version of
the 'homebred country girl', insisting that Emily was
an 'unobtrusive' woman, whose 'perfectly secluded life'
emphasised her 'retiring manners and habits' (WH, 35).
On the other hand, Emily is presented as the type of
the Romantic genius – eccentric, larger than life, and not
bound by the usual constraints that govern Charlotte's and
her contemporary audience's conception of the feminine:
'I have never seen her parallel in anything. Stronger than
a man, simpler than a child, her nature stood alone'
(WH, 35). Charlotte Brontë's inability to understand
and account for her sister's life and work in terms of
early-Victorian definitions of the feminine, and of female
writing, leads her to represent Emily as a polarised and
divided self.

> In Emily's nature the extremes of vigour and simplicity
> seemed to meet. Under an unsophisticated culture, inarti-
> ficial tastes, and an unpretending outside, lay a secret
> power and fire that might have informed the brain and
> kindled the veins of a hero. (WH, 35)

It would seem that Charlotte could only understand her sister, and account for her literary power, by seeing her, as many later critics have, as a doubly atypical woman. On the one hand, Emily's unworldliness and lack of social intercourse render her views less judicious and comprehensive than those of more experienced and worldly women, while, on the other, her 'secret power and fire' places her on the margins of her gender as a potential 'hero'. In fact the literary power of Emily's poems seems to take her out of the female gender altogether, as in Charlotte Brontë's view, 'these were not common effusions, not at all like the poetry women generally write' (WH, 30). This latter judgement reveals Charlotte to be bound by the same critical double standard which motivated the Brontë sisters to adopt their pseudonyms of Currer, Ellis and Acton Bell. They eschewed the use of those male pseudonyms whose widespread adoption, Elaine Showalter has argued, indicates a 'radical understanding of the role playing required by women's effort to participate in the main stream of literary culture',[5] and opted for gender-neutral pseudonyms, an 'ambiguous choice', as Charlotte Brontë noted, which was

> dictated by a sort of conscientious scruple at assuming Christian names positively masculine, while we did not like to declare ourselves women, because – without at the time suspecting that our mode of writing and thinking was not what is called 'feminine' – we had a vague impression that authoresses are liable to be looked on with prejudice; we had noticed how critics sometimes use for their chastisement the weapon of personality, and for their reward, a flattery, which is not true praise. (WH, 31)

Charlotte's account raises the issue of the critical double standard and the separate spheres, two of the most serious problems which faced the woman writer in the eighteenth and nineteenth centuries (and which have not entirely disappeared in our own day). Despite, or perhaps because of, the growing number of women writers – particularly novelists – in the late eighteenth and early nineteenth century, many commentators still thought that writing for a living was an intrinsically unwomanly activity. When Charlotte Brontë sent some of her poems to Robert Southey in 1837 she was sternly reminded that 'literature cannot be the business of a woman's life, and it ought not to be. The more she is engaged in her proper duties, the less leisure she will have for it' (LL I, 155). Even in 1850 George Henry Lewes offered this 'Gentle Hint to Writing Women':

> Women's proper sphere of activity is elsewhere. Are there no husbands, lovers, brothers, friends to coddle and console? Are there no stockings to darn, no purses to make, no braces to embroider? *My* idea of a perfect woman is one who can write but won't.[6]

Those women who persisted in writing and succeeded in publishing their works, found them subjected to different critical criteria from those applied to the writings of men. According to George Eliot, an extremely successful woman writer, the critical standards applied to women writers were inimical to originality and ability. 'By a peculiar thermometric adjustment, when a woman's talent is at zero, journalistic approbation is at the boiling pitch . . . and if ever she reaches excellence, critical enthusiasm drops to freezing point'.[7] Reviews of books by women tended to concentrate on the author's femininity, and unless she adopted a masculine pseudonym, a woman writer would automatically be ranked with other women writers no matter how diverse their subject matter or style.

Quite simply, female writers and male writers were held to inhabit separate creative spheres, a doctrine which, in effect, was a doctrine of limitation for women novelists, confining them to a limited range of subject matter and a limited register of language. The power of the ideology of the separate spheres is evident in Charlotte's 'defence' of her sister's achievement. Ironically, Charlotte Brontë, who was herself to play such an important part in redefining and expanding the domain of female fiction, is forced in her Biographical Notice to construct a defence of her sister's work within the terms of the prevailing view of the proper sphere of the female novelist, as she attempts to account for literary works which are not simply extraordinary, but which are also 'unwomanly' – in the sense that they transgress the socially accepted code of the 'feminine'.

Of course, Charlotte is not alone among those who knew Emily in remarking upon her strangeness and her power. Nor is she the only commentator to attempt to account for those qualities by finding Emily an extraordinary woman, entirely untypical of her gender. For example, when M. Héger, the Brontës' teacher in Brussels, gave his recollections of the author of *Wuthering Heights* to Elizabeth Gaskell, he did not remember the 'ignorant' and 'timid' girl who figured in his school reports, but recalled instead an extraordinary young woman who should have been a man – a great navigator whose

> powerful reason would have deduced new spheres of discovery from the knowledge of the old; and her strong, imperious will would never have been daunted by opposition or difficulty; never have given way but with life . . . her faculty of imagination was such that, if she had written a history, her view of scenes and characters would have been so vivid, and so powerfully expressed, and supported by such a show of argument, that it would have dominated over the reader, whatever might have been his previous opinions, or his cooler perceptions of its truth. (quoted, WG, 127)

Even more interesting than the radical revision of M. Heger's initial opinion of Emily's timidity is the nature of the language which he uses to describe his sense of her qualities. His admiration for Emily's imagination, reason, argumentative skill, resilience and determination can only, it seems, be expressed in terms of a masculine language of domination. Emily Brontë repeatedly poses this problem to commentators caught in this linguistic and cultural trap. Male discourse is not simply the dominant discourse, it is also a discourse of domination in which originality, argumentative *power, force* of reason etc. are linguistically represented as masculine qualities. The woman who possesses such 'powers' is thus almost inevitably spoken of as masculine. Hence, Emily 'should have been a man', she is nicknamed 'The Major' and serves as the model for Charlotte's ambiguously named heroine Shirley (who refers to herself as 'Captain Keeldar'), and she is the stuff of which 'heroes' are made.

One of the few commentators to convey an admiration of Emily's originality, strength and forcefulness without simultaneously suggesting that these powers unwomanned her was John Greenwood, the Haworth stationer, who left a diary of events in Haworth. On the contrary, Greenwood presents Emily's power and strength, of which he provides some startling examples, in terms of a language of competence and practicality. In other words, Emily's power is expressed not simply as *dominance* but also as *ability*. For example, in the following episode, resourcefulness and quick-thinking are just as important as physical force, and although Emily's actions outshine the men of the village, they do not make her a superman:

> On one occasion a person went to tell them that Keeper [Emily's dog] and another great powerful dog out of the village were fighting . . . She never spoke a word, nor appeared the least at a loss what to do, but rushed at once

into the kitchen, took the pepper box, and away into the lane, where she found the two savage brutes each holding the other by the throat . . . while several other animals, who thought themselves men, were standing looking like cowards . . . watching this fragile creature spring upon the beasts – seizing Keeper round the neck with one arm, while with the other hand she dredges well their noses with pepper, and separating them by force of her great will . . . (WG, 146–7)

It is salutary to be reminded of the 'fragile creature' concealed behind the superwoman/man of literary legend, or, in another of Greenwood's stories, of the outwardly dutiful daughter who alternated pistol practice with baking. For, while Emily Brontë's life and work define themselves against the limitations of prevailing nineteenth-century ideas of the female lot and women's creativity, they also expand and explore those boundaries. By retreating ever further within the limits of domestic life Emily Brontë created a space from which to explore those limitations. By retreating ever further into the 'dream-worlds' of her fictional creations she was able to experiment with alternative visions of reality in which dominance, power, and energy are not exclusively masculine qualities, and nor do they necessarily prevail.

2 The Writings of Ellis Bell

Just as Emily Brontë eludes the biographer's attempts to grasp the details of her life, and to reconcile the conflicting versions of the woman that she was, so too her work resists definition and categorisation. Nevertheless, in this chapter I shall attempt to suggest some recurring themes and preoccupations in Brontë's writings, and to explore the relationship of her work to contemporary writing by both men and women.

The elusiveness of Emily Brontë's work derives, in part, from the fact that it offers a variety of voices and guises. Charlotte Brontë's Biographical Memoir recalls her sister's enthusiasm for her persona of Ellis Bell, and 'Bell's' writings in turn reveal a dramatic writer who experimented with a variety of alternative selves.

Emily Brontë's fictions are almost always dramatic in form. In *Wuthering Heights*, for example, the author eschews the role of omniscient narrator, or the confessional mode of the first person narrative favoured by her sister Charlotte, building her narrative instead on a complex structure of dramatised first person narratives, letters, and diaries. The form of the poems too is, broadly speaking, dramatic. The Gondal poems, and what little we are able to reconstruct of their context in the Gondal narrative, reveal Emily Brontë as a chameleon poet, creating and experimenting with a variety of dramatised situations, moods and emotions. This is not to say that the Gondal poems are thoroughly dramatised in the manner, for example, of the dramatic poems of the later Victorian poet Robert Browning. The Gondal characters are not so much discrete dramatic creations as alternative selves, which offer opportunities for the kind of ventriloquism suggested by the 1845 Birthday Paper's description of an excursion with Anne, during which

> we were Rosalind Macalgin, Henry Angora, Juliet
> Angusteena, Rosabella Esmalden, Ella and Julian Egre-
> mont, Catherine Navarre, and Cordelia Fitzaphnold
> escaping from the palaces of instruction to join the
> Royalists who are hard driven at present by the Victorious
> Republicans. The Gondals still flourish as bright as ever.
> (LL II, 49–50)

Emily Brontë's non-Gondal work is no less dramatic, but in these poems she does not so much experiment with alternative selves as seek to create or articulate a viable self in the face of the versions of the self she found in the work of the male poets of the Romantic tradition. This was a tradition in which it was difficult for women to participate, as Margaret Homans has noted, 'not for constitutional reasons but for reasons that women readers found within the literature itself'.[1] In the Romantic tradition woman inspires poetry, either as Muse or as a feminised Nature, but she does not write it, because she is excluded from the role of 'speaking subject' which is identified as male.

Indeed, in general terms, the liberating project of the male Romantic writers was profoundly problematic for women. The Romantic writers' preoccupation with individualism, self-expression, and a soaring freedom of the spirit did not accord with the social and psychological situations of most women. Thus to see Emily Brontë's dramatic ventriloquism as a means of enacting her 'megalomaniac fantasy', as Rosalind Miles does,[2] is to ignore the realities of the situation of women, and particularly of writing women, in the early nineteenth century. A woman who sought power at this time was not power crazed, but was seeking to remedy a lack. Brontë's alternative selves might more usefully be seen as executive selves, venturing into landscapes and experiences from which, as the Victorian daughter of the vicarage, she was debarred. They are imaginative attempts to overcome the limitations of actual experience and are, in this more limited sense, the enactment or embodiment of their creator's fantasies of power.

The dramatic guises and alternative selves of Emily Brontë's poems and novel are part of her constant attempt to transcend the limitations of a female lot that is 'at present too straitly-bounded',[3] and if we should seek to locate the creative impulse of her work in any single source we might locate it not as C. Day Lewis did in her supposed frustrations at not being a man,[4] but rather in her frustration with the cultural limitations which constrained women. Almost all of Emily Brontë's writings are centrally concerned with the transcending of these and other limitations, and with the dissolving of boundaries. Imprisonment and the yearning for release, restraint and freedom are key oppositions which provide a central dynamic of both her novel and poems.

Actual prisons form the dramatic settings for a number of the Gondal poems, whose characters languish in dark dungeons, exiled from their former lives, chafing against their bonds, seeking to escape them either literally or imaginatively in memories or images of liberty, or, as in this early poem, where cold harsh imprisonment is remembered from the soaring vantage point of restored liberty.

> O god of heaven! the dream of horror,
> The frightful dream is over now;
> The sickened heart, the blasting sorrow,
> The ghastly night, the ghastlier morrow,
> The aching sense of utter woe.
> . . .
> It's over now – and I am free,
> And the ocean wind is caressing me,
> The wild wind from the wavy main
> . . .
> Shake off the fetters, break the chain,
> And live and love and smile again

> The waste of youth, the waste of years,
> Departed in that dongeon's thrall;
> The gnawing grief, the hopeless tears,
> Forget them – O forget them all.
>
> (H 15, 40–1)[5]

The bondage of the spirit in the limitations of physical and earthly existence, and the desire to transcend these limitations, again through memory and imagination, and sympathetic identification with the natural world are also central concerns of both the Gondal poems and the more personal poems. The wind and exalting images of a free nature are the most frequent antitheses to images of restraint and limitation as in 'High waving heather'.

> High waving heather, 'neath stormy blasts bending,
> Midnight and moonlight and bright shining stars;
> Darkness and glory rejoicingly blending,
> Earth rising to heaven and heaven descending,
> Man's spirit away from its drear dongeon sending,
> Bursting the fetters and breaking the bars.
>
> (H 5, 31)

Another important source of power and liberty is the imagination, with its capacity to transcend 'Nature's sad reality'.

> So hopeless is the world without,
> The world within I doubly prize,
> The world where guile and hate and doubt
> And cold suspicion never rise;
> Where thou and I and Liberty
> Have undisputed sovereignty.
>
> (H 174, 205-6)

Many of Emily Brontë's poems explore and celebrate the self-transcendence achieved by the willing surrender to those 'hovering visions' of the imagination which can burst the fetters and break the bars that imprison the soul in the body.

> I'm happiest when most away
> I can bear my soul from its home of clay
> On a windy night when the moon is bright
> And the eye can wander through worlds of light –
>
> When I am not and none beside –
> Nor earth nor sea nor cloudless sky –
> But only spirit wandering wide
> Through infinite immensity.

(H 44, 63)

Spiritual constraint and physical restriction or incarceration also figure prominently in *Wuthering Heights*. Catherine and Heathcliff most obviously represent their creator's fascination with imprisoned souls who chafe against the limitations of physical and earthly existence, and the best-remembered words of this memorable novel, 'Nelly I am Heathcliff', place the question of boundaries and the desire to transcend them firmly at its centre. *Wuthering Heights* is also centrally concerned with the social, psychological and spiritual imprisonment of its characters, particularly its female characters, who are depicted as being imprisoned within the power relations of a patriarchal legal system (on which much of the plot turns), and by systems of cultural oppression such as the prevailing notion of the genteel lady. The novel also investigates the imprisoning force of religion, in the severely judgemental Calvinism of Joseph, and through its interrogation of the view of woman as sinful Eve.

Although, even at its lowest point, Wuthering Heights

cannot be compared to the dark, dank dungeons of
the Gondal poems, nevertheless both the Heights and
Thrushcross Grange are presented as prisons. Isabella,
Linton Heathcliff, and the second Catherine are all at
various stages literally incarcerated at the Heights. At other
times the two domestic settings of the novel are presented as
psychological prisons, particularly, though not exclusively,
for the female characters. Imprisonment, whether psychological, spiritual or physical, is of course an important
metaphor in the novels of both male and female Victorian
writers. In the novels of the Brontë sisters, however, the
heroine's physical confinement 'often reflects her sense of
spiritual imprisonment in a hostile environment which is
shaped and controlled by men'.[6] Recent feminist critics have
also seen Emily Brontë's 'concern with spatial constrictions',
and 'imagery of enclosure',[7] as characteristic of a specifically
female version of the Gothic novel. Indeed, some feminist
critics have argued that the Gothic is a peculiarly female
sub-genre of the novel, whose 'eccentricities' have been
seen 'as indigenous to "woman's fantasy" '.[8] Sandra Gilbert
and Susan Gubar have suggested some of the reasons why
this is so.

> literally confined to the house, figuratively confined
> to a single 'place,' enclosed in parlours and encased in
> texts, imprisoned in kitchens and enshrined in stanzas,
> women artists naturally found themselves describing
> dark interiors and confusing their sense that they
> were house-bound with their rebellion against being
> duty bound. (Gilbert and Gubar (a), 84)

The Gothic novel – a genre in which 'fantasy predomi-
nates over reality, the strange over the commonplace, and
the supernatural over the natural' (Moers, 90) – enjoyed
something of a cult status in the latter part of the
eighteenth century. The cult of the Gothic novel in

English began with Hugh Walpole's *The Castle of Otranto* (1765), but perhaps its most influential exponent was Ann Radcliffe, whose *The Mysteries of Udolpho* (1794) is widely regarded as the quintessential Gothic novel. In the hands of Ann Radcliffe and her numerous imitators, Gothic became a powerful form for shaping female experience and fantasies, a form that not only 'unleashed the imagination, but [also] made it possible to show women acting boldly on their own behalf, with fortitude and courage' (Figes, 61). At the same time Gothic offered a form of travel and adventure which accorded with the socially constrained circumstances of a woman's life – 'indoor travel' –

> indoors, in the long twisting passageways of the Gothic castle, there is travel with danger, travel with exertion – a challenge to the heroine's enterprize, resolution, ingenuity and physical strength . . . It was *only* indoors, in Mrs. Radcliffe's day, that the heroine of a novel could travel brave and free, and stay respectable. (Moers, 129)

In *Wuthering Heights*, as I shall show in a later chapter, Emily Brontë both modernises and domesticates Gothic. In place of high-born maidens in distress in Bluebeards' castles in exotic foreign locations, she follows the adventures of the daughters of Yorkshire yeomanry and gentry in ostensibly ordinary farmhouses and small, country houses.

In Emily Brontë's poems, images of constriction and restraint have their antithesis in images of a free and soaring nature, or a spirit that soars free of nature. Similarly, in her novel, imprisoning domestic interiors, whether savagely inhospitable or suffocatingly genteel, have as their antithesis the free untramelled nature of the moors. Limitless space is the liberating or, in some cases, hazardous alternative to domestic enclosure. Another important element of the novel's central dynamic of freedom and restraint is its dramatisation and investigation of various strategies of escape, both positive and negative, creative and destructive. In the case of most of the female characters, attempts to escape their psychological or physical imprisonment usually result merely in exchanging one form of imprisonment for another. Such is the case with the cross-migrations of the two Catherines and Isabella from the Heights to the Grange. The predicament of these characters seems to involve that semantic problem which is dramatically illustrated in Jane Eyre's desperate recognition that terms such as 'liberty', 'change', 'stimulus' are not attached to stable and sustainable meanings within female experience, but float off into a vacuum which can only be filled and given definition in terms of a 'new servitude'.

> I desired liberty; for liberty I gasped; for liberty I uttered a prayer; it seemed scattered on the wind then faintly blowing. I abandoned it and formed a humbler supplication; for change, stimulus; that petition, too, seemed swept off into vague space: 'Then' I cried, half desperate, 'grant me at least a new servitude!'[9]

Another self-destructive form of the attempt to escape the social and psychological constraints of the female lot is figured in the various wasting illnesses of the female characters, or of feminised characters such as Linton Heathcliff. Frances Earnshaw and Isabella Linton-Heathcliff both waste away under the pressures of female existence which proved fatal to so many women characters in Victorian fiction, and which were indeed severely incapacitating for many Victorian women. The closing stages of Catherine Earnshaw's life seem to offer a classic illustration of the tendency of some nineteenth-century women novelists to 'create characters who attempt to escape, if only into nothingness, through the suicidal self-starvation of anorexia' (Gilbert and Gubar (a), 85).

If this latter strategy is a somewhat self-defeating image

of escape, an escape through the keyhole of the prison door,
or, in Catherine's case an escape through the prison window,
Emily Brontë's writings also offer alternative and more
positive images of freedom in the form of images of female
power. In A.G.A., the Queen of Gondal, she provides a
powerful female alternative to the Byronic and militaristic
male characters of Charlotte and Branwell's Angrian
chronicles. The leader of Charlotte Brontë's fictional
kingdom, Arthur Wellesley, 'an arch-Byronic hero, for
love of whom noble ladies went into romantic decline', has
his mirror-image in Emily Brontë's Gondal's queen, who

> was of such compelling beauty and charm as to bring all
> men to her feet, and of such selfish cruelty as to bring
> tragedy to all who loved her . . . It was as if Emily was
> saying to Charlotte, 'You think the man is the dominant
> factor in romantic love, I'll show you it is the woman.'[10]

The following lines on the outlawed Angelica suggest
what is involved in this image of female power.

> One was a woman, tall and fair;
> A princess she might be,
> From her stately form, and her features rare,
> And her look of majesty.
>
> But, oh, she had a sullen frown,
> A lip of cruel scorn,
> As sweet tears never melted down
> Her cheeks since she was born!
>   . . .
> And he was noble too, who bowed
> So humbly by her side,
> Entreating, till his eyes o'erflowed,
> Her spirit's icy pride.

(H 143, 151)

Wuthering Heights produces its own distinctive and differentiated images of female power in the two Catherines, and in the resourceful and independent Nelly Dean. Moreover, in its particular handling of the love plots, it creates 'a world where men battle for the favours of apparently high-spirited and independent women' (Gilbert and Gubar (a), 249).

Brontë's 'high-spirited and independent women' are also important vehicles for her exploration of the nature and sources of selfhood. In the poems a concern with self-integrity, fidelity to an essential selfhood, and a desire to be

> True to myself, and true to all
> May I be healthful still,
> And turn away from passion's call
> And curb my own wild will,
>
> (H 10, 35)

alternates with a fear of self-alienation, and a dramatised exploration of the process of exile from the self. In *Wuthering Heights*, Catherine's contention that Heathcliff is 'more myself than I am' raises central questions about the nature, sources, and boundaries of the self. Catherine's persistent desire to go back, to re-unite with the lost self of childhood, with Nature, or with her alienated spirit, is constantly echoed in the characters or lyrical voices of the poems. In the case of Catherine and Heathcliff in particular, the state of adulthood is seen as 'a condition of forfeit and exile',[11] while the poems are pervaded by images of regression, and by nostalgia for a half-forgotten past.

In many cases the yearning to be restored to a more integrated former selfhood is accompanied by a sense of loss and forgetfulness which is specifically related to the activity of writing. 'Alone I sat', for example, rehearses a sense of frustrated poetic vocation in terms of an inability to make the dreams of the past, present in language.

"Dreams have encircled me," I said,
"From careless childhood's sunny time,
Visions by ardent fancy fed
Since life was in its prime."
. . .
But now, when I had hoped to sing,
My fingers strike a tuneless string;
And still the burden of the strain
Is "Strive no more; 'tis all in vain."
                                        (H 27, 49)

The sense of failure in these lines is a kind of forgetfulness;
the visions endure, the writer retains the Wordsworthian
ability to be 'affected by absent things as if they were
present' ('Preface' to *Lyrical Ballads*), but the songs that
accompanied the visions have been forgotten, as in Christina
Rossetti's 'The Key-Note'.

Where are the songs I used to know,
Where are the notes I used to sing?
I have forgotten everything
I used to know so long ago.

It has been suggested that such forgetfulness is a condition
specific to female writers whose 'deep sense of alienation
and inescapable feeling of anomie' is linked to the feeling
'that they have forgotten something' (Gilbert and Gubar
(a), 58–9)

One of the things from which Emily Brontë's personae
have become estranged, and which they constantly seek
to recover, is a sense of a vital connection with nature.
Notwithstanding her problematic relationship to certain
of the projects and positions of male Romantic writers,
Emily Brontë nevertheless shares many of their concerns,
and in some cases was directly influenced by them. Like
Wordsworth, Emily Brontë was something of a nature

mystic, although the 'sense of something far more deeply interfused' ('Tintern Abbey') that she perceives in nature is usually less ordered and moralised than in Wordsworth.

Wuthering Heights also has its Wordsworthian aspects. Brontë's choice of setting, her plotting, and some aspects of characterisation are indebted to *Lyrical Ballads*, and to the ballad tradition upon which Wordsworth drew. Interestingly, both Charlotte and Emily Brontë seem to have associated the ballad tradition with women, and Ellen Dean, like Bessie in *Jane Eyre*, is portrayed as the custodian and transmitter of a vital and vitalising oral culture, and of a shared communal experience.

As well as being indebted to the popular tradition of ballads, and that tradition as rewritten for 'polite' audiences by Scott and Wordsworth, Emily Brontë was also clearly influenced by other male Romantic poets, most notably Byron and Shelley. Indeed, she seems constantly to have been rewriting Shelley's 'Ode to the West Wind', most notably in 'Aye, there it is! It wakes tonight!', which ends with a Shelleyan Platonic vision of the soul escaping from the imprisoning body.

> Yes, I could swear that glorious wind
> Has swept the world aside,
> Has dashed its memory from thy mind
> Like foam-bells from the tide –
> . . .
> Thus truly when that breast is cold
> Thy prisoned soul shall rise,
> The dungeon mingle with the mould –
> The captive with the skies.
>
> (H 148, 165)

Brontë's recurring preoccupation wth the imprisoned soul and the neglected captive may be traced, at least in part, to Shelley's *Epipsychidion* (1821), a poem in

honour of platonic love, addressed to the 'poor captive
bird' Emilia Viviani, who at nineteen was incarcerated in
a convent while her parents conducted negotiations for her
marriage. Brontë's depiction of Catherine and Heathcliff is
prefigured in Shelley's vision of a transcendent love which
cannot

> . . . be constrained, it overleaps all fence:
> Like lightning, with invisible violence
> Piercing its continent. . .
>   (*Epipsychidion*, 1583ff.)

Like all of the Brontës, Emily was also profoundly
influenced by Byron. Her proud, defiant heroes and
heroines, her fascination with bandits, outlaws, prisoners,
exiles, and other rootless characters of mysterious origin
all owe a great deal to Byron, as do some of her favourite
settings and landscapes. But, most importantly, in Byron
Emily Brontë found 'the champion of unsociable man' (WG,
46), unconventional, lawless, proud, wilful, independent,
and rebellious. Here, her reading of Byron interlocks with
her reading of Milton – her father's favourite poet. The
Byronic heroes of *Wuthering Heights* and the poems owe a
great deal to Emily Brontë's profound fascination with the
thwarted power of the Satan of *Paradise Lost*.

Emily Brontë, like her brother and sisters, was also
an avid reader of *Blackwood's Edinburgh Magazine*, which
was a major vehicle for the dissemination of Romantic
fiction, publishing and reviewing numerous works of the
horror school which derived from German tales and early
Byron. In the pages of 'Maga' Emily Brontë would have
encountered examples or discussions of the work of Mary
Shelley, E.T.A. Hoffman, and James Hogg, each of whom
experimented with the tale of evil-possession, and with the
theme of the *doppelgänger*, described by a *Blackwood's*
reviewer in July 1824 as a

visitation of another self, a double with a man's own
personal appearance, who in his name, and in his likeness,
commits every atrocious crime of which he would never
have believed himself capable.

Typically the hero, or hero-villain of such fiction is
remarkable for his inhuman nature, and it is clear that
Heathcliff and some of the Gondalian characters belong,
at least in part, to this genre.

James Hogg's *The Private Memoirs and Confessions of a
Justified Sinner* (published anonymously in 1824) offers a
particularly interesting version of the *doppelgänger* theme,
and was much discussed in *Blackwood's*. Hogg makes his
extraordinary tale all the more powerful by setting it, like
Wuthering Heights, in an unextraordinary, everyday world,
and his use of a divided narrative also anticipates Brontë's
choice of narrative method.

Mary Shelley's *Valperga* (1823) also contains a prototype
Heathcliff in Castruccio, a previously gentle man, who
has been transformed into a cruel tyrant. Moreover, one
of Castruccio's victims, the diabolic Beatrice of Ferrara,
expounds a vision of 'the eternal and victorious influence of
evil which circulates in the air around us', which is echoed
in Emily Brontë's fictional writings, and in the essays she
wrote for M. Heger.

La nature est un probleme inexplicable, elle existe
sur un principe de destruction; il faut que tout être
soit l'instrument infatigable de mort aux autres . . . en
ce moment l'univers me paraissait une vaste machine
construite seulement pour produire la mal. (WG, 272)

Beatrice's view of the universe also has similarities with
an important strand of *Wuthering Heights*:

'reflect on domestic life, on the strife, hatred and

uncharitableness that pierces one's bosom at every
turn . . . Oh! surely God's hand is the chastening
hand of a father that thus torments his children! He
created man – that most wretched of slaves; Oh! know
you not what a wretch man is! and what a store-house
of infinite pain in this much-vaunted human soul? Look
into your own heart . . . or gaze on mine; I will tear it
open for your inspection. There is hatred, remorse, grief
– overwhelming night, and eternal misery'.

The *Blackwood's* reviewer of *Valperga* quoted the above
lines as an example of how women ought *not* to write.
Such writing belonged

to a *certain* school which is certainly a very modern
as well as a very mischievous one, and which ought
never, of all things, to have numbered ladies among
its disciples. (*Blackwood's*, March 1823)

The independent pupil revealed in the French *devoirs*
Emily Brontë wrote for M. Heger was clearly full of such
unladylike tendencies, as was the creator of Heathcliff,
Catherine, and the first Hareton Earnshaw. The poems
too, articulate their own vision of the way things are,
which cannot be contained by the *Blackwood's* reviewer's
conception of the ladylike – the dominant view of early
nineteenth-century culture.

If in her choice of form, and in many of her central
preoccupations, Emily Brontë seems to have been a retrospective novelist who looks back to the Romantic tradition
of the tale of horror, the novel of evil-possession, and to
the Gothic tradition, she also shares many of the concerns
of the emerging Victorian novelists. Indeed, in a sense, the
retrospective tendency of her fiction mirrors the Victorian
novelists' concern with the recent past. Many of the Victorian novelists looked back to Wordsworth and developed

his autobiographical impulse, his interest in the growth and development of the individual in a specific time and place, his documenting of the 'incidents of common life', and particularly his depiction of the customs and manners of a vanishing pattern of rural life. In addition much Victorian fiction shares Sir Walter Scott's interest in the romance of the past, and in the processes of historical change. *Wuthering Heights* was just one of a number of Victorian novels which learned valuable lessons from Scott's interest in regional dialect, folklore, local custom and the ballad tradition.

Like Scott's novels and *The Lyrical Ballads*, *Wuthering Heights* brings together realism and romance, two modes which co-exist in a state of dynamic tension in much Victorian fiction. The 'real', as Henry James observed in his Preface to *The American*, denotes 'the things we cannot possibly *not* know sooner or later', whereas the romantic concerns 'the things that can reach us only through the beautiful circuit and subterfuge of our own thought and desire'.[12]

Female writers had more reason than their male counterparts for acknowledging the power of the real, but partly because of the limitations of their lot, and partly because of their access to alternative traditions, they also had more reason to keep open the door 'to the transforming energies of romance, with its "subterfuge" promise that life might be shaped to the heart's desire'.[13] By taking the diabolic characters, *doppelgängers*, spirits, and extreme passions of the tales of horror, and transposing them to the vividly realised setting of the domestic life of the inhabitants of the Yorkshire moors in the recent past, Emily Brontë simultaneously explores the relationship between the real and the 'beautiful . . . subterfuge of . . . desire', and domesticates Gothic in a manner which accommodates romance to the emerging domestic realism of the Victorian novel.

However, while *Wuthering Heights'* domestication of Gothic takes it in the direction of an emerging Victorian domestic realism, it does so in a revisionary form, which provides a powerful critique of both domesticity and realism. Moreover, although it is important to attempt to see the novel in and of its time, it is also equally important to acknowledge the ways in which it resists prevailing fictional practice. For example, in its lack of overt didacticism *Wuthering Heights* marks itself off from the developing tradition of Victorian fiction, and indeed from a central tradition of female writing. Whatever one makes of the novel's treatment of the second generation characters and their 'happy ending' in marriage and domesticity, it is nevertheless impossible to fit *Wuthering Heights* neatly into that tradition of rational, improving literature which was developed by women writers, from the eighteenth century onwards. *Wuthering Heights* also resists the religious didacticism which is particularly associated with novels by women. Indeed, in some senses *Wuthering Heights* seems to be an anti-religious novel which presents most conventional religious positions as both imaginatively and morally limited and limiting. The novel certainly adopts unconventional positions towards religion, and looks forward to D.H. Lawrence's religion of the blood, on the one hand, and back to the visions of William Blake, on the other.

Finally, in *Wuthering Heights* Emily Brontë signally declined to ally herself with that specifically Victorian development of the didactic novel (which was taken up by many women writers) – the social problem novel. In general Emily Brontë's writings seem markedly unconcerned with the immediate issues of the day. At a time when other novelists were seeking to develop a form which could articulate the experience of living in a modern urban, industrial world, and when they were addressing the social and political problems of such a civilisation, Emily Brontë wrote an 'old-fashioned' novel which was, nevertheless, 'fifty years ahead of its time in its radical indeterminacy'.[14]

Emily Brontë's work, in some respects, demonstrates the dilemma of the central figure in Matthew Arnold's 'Stanzas From the Grand Chartreuse',

> Wandering between two worlds, one dead,
> The other powerless to be born.

In her efforts to write, Emily Brontë 'wanders' between past and present, Romantic and Victorian, realism and romance; she steers a path between the dominant male tradition and the marginalised female tradition, between the largely female tradition of didactic fiction, which invoked duty to God, the family and the community, and the alternative traditions of Gothic and a poetic of the free spirit. Out of the struggle to find her own place and voice comes the work which we shall examine in detail in the following pages.

3 'Not at all like the poetry women generally write': the Problem of the Woman Poet

> The other option's to become a bird.
> That's kindly done, to guess from how they sing,
> decently independent of the word
> as we are not; and how they use the air
> to sail as we might soaring on a swing
> higher and higher; but the rope's not there,
>
> (Fleur Adcock, 'A Way Out')

In a letter of 1845 Elizabeth Barrett Browning lamented that 'England has had many learned women . . . and yet where are the poetesses? . . . I look everywhere for grandmothers, and see none'.[1] In the following year the absence of English poetesses was in some measure rectified by the publication of *Poems by Currer, Ellis and Acton Bell*,[2] which contained twenty one poems by Emily Brontë. This volume sold only two copies, and received few immediate critical notices; nevertheless its publication heralded the arrival of one of the few pre-twentieth-century female poets to be admitted to the canon of English poetry. However, although Emily Brontë was to become one of the 'grandmothers' whose lack Elizabeth Barrett Browning had felt to be so constraining to the aspiring woman writer, her work also demonstrates the difficulties of being one's own grandmother, that is to say, of writing without or against a literary tradition.

This aspect of Emily Brontë's work raises in acute form the 'problem of the woman poet', both in the sense of the problems experienced by the woman who aspires to write poetry, and of the problem the woman poet has presented to traditional literary criticism. In order to explore both of these problems I want to look at Emily Brontë's poems in relation to the context in which they were produced, and also in relation to the contexts in which Emily Brontë has been produced as a poet, that is to say, the ways in which she has been read.

Emily Brontë's poetry provides a very interesting case study of a particular woman in a particular time, place, and culture, trying to work within particular poetic conventions, and particular definitions of poetry. The following lines by Jane Ransome Biddell suggest something of the nature of the problematic within which Brontë wrote and was read.

> Ideal forms no longer glide
> In dreaming mood before my view
> As nesting round my own fire side
> I see a little laughing crew. . .
>
> But not a muse my call attends,
> They shun the dear domestic hearth
> And inspiration still descends
> On spirits more detached from earth.[3]

These two stanzas juxtapose profoundly ideological versions of the feminine role and the nature of the poet. They starkly and poignantly embody the conflict between the domestic ideology, with its emphasis on the self-sacrificing rewards of motherhood, and the Romantic view of the poet as an inspired and aspiring spirit detached from worldly cares and responsibilities. Emily Brontë's poetry persistently dramatises and demonstrates the difficulties experienced by the woman poet faced with the task of trying to negotiate the constraints of a Romantic conception of poetry which seems to exclude women as defined in nineteenth-century society.

Charlotte Brontë's story of her discovery of Emily's poems and the subsequent publication of the slim volume of poems by the Brontë sisters is well known, but it is worth retelling in order to remind ourselves not only of Emily Brontë's intensely, almost compulsively private nature, but also of the circumstances in which she wrote.

> One day, in the autumn of 1845, I accidentally lighted on a MS. volume of verse in my sister Emily's handwriting. Of course, I was not surprised, knowing that she could and did write verse; I looked it over, and something more than surprise seized me – a deep conviction that these were not common effusions, nor at all like the poetry women generally write. I thought them condensed and terse, vigorous and genuine. To my ear, they also had a peculiar music – wild, melancholy, and elevating.
>
> . . . It took hours to reconcile her to the discovery I had made, and days to persuade her that such poems merited publication. I knew, however, that a mind like hers could not be without some latent spark of honourable ambition, and refused to be discouraged in my attempts to fan that spark into flame. (WH, 31)

If we are to believe Charlotte's account – and despite her tendency towards myth making, there is no reason to doubt her essential veracity – Emily Brontë was a secret, even secretive, writer of poetry. She did not attempt to conceal the fact that she could and sometimes did write verse, but she apparently concealed from her sisters both the nature of the poetry she wrote, and her *commitment* to the activity of writing poetry. In fact the subject matter of many of her poems, as well as the evidence of brief autobiographical statements, suggest that writing was not simply a genteel diversion for Emily Brontë but was the central activity of her life.

On the whole, later critics have echoed Charlotte Brontë's view of the extraordinariness of her sister's poems, particularly her feeling that they were not 'at all like the poetry women generally write'. Charlotte presumably had in mind the kind of women's poetry characterised by Cora Kaplan as being concerned with 'domestic pleasures, the comforts of religion, the beauty of sunsets and the effects – but not the causes – of the discontents that led them to write poetry in the first place'.[4]

In contrast, Emily Brontë's poetry has been valued for its originality, intensity, power, sternness, plainness, and its lyric force. For example, T. Wemyss Reid, in 1877, found her verse 'strong, calm, sincere' (CH, 398), while Swinburne admired the 'plain-song note of Emily's clear, stern verse' (CH, 411–12). Significantly these qualities were considered to be unusual, not to say unique, in a woman poet. Emily Brontë's poems were, and in some quarters still are, considered remarkable precisely because they were unlike 'the spasmodic and frothy outpourings of Byron-stricken girls' (T.W. Reid, CH, 398), and because she 'escaped the worn formalities of much early nineteenth-century poetry by women'[5] – what a recent feminist critic has described as the 'dribbling treacle of women's verse'.[6] There seems to be a perverse logic operating in this general judgement. Emily Brontë is a good poet because her work is untypical of women poets. How and why is she untypical of women poets? Because she is good!

Although the perceived 'unwomanliness' of Emily Brontë's verse has saved her from the oblivion to which most women poets have been consigned by literary history, at least until the relatively recent attempts of feminist critics to re-examine and redefine literary traditions, nevertheless, Emily Brontë's place in the poetic canon has been a minor one, which she owes to a handful of 'really great' poems – as few as a half-dozen according to Derek Stanford.[7] Others have been more generous in their assessments of what is

worth saving, but there seems to be general agreement that
Emily Brontë wrote a great deal of bad or unimportant
poetry, much of which is connected with the fictional
kingdom of Gondal which she created in childhood, and
whose history she continued to elaborate until the end of
her life.

The Importance of Gondal

Clearly, by 1844, when she began transcribing her finished
poems into two separate notebooks – one headed 'Gondal
Poems', the other untitled – the poet herself made some
kind of distinction between the Gondal and non-Gondal
aspects of her work, and she certainly suppressed all
references to the Gondal narrative in the poems published
in 1846. Critical opinion has been sharply divided about
the role, significance, and value of the Gondal poems, and
of the whole Gondal element in Emily Brontë's work. My
interest in the Gondal poems and in the critical debate they
have generated lies not in what they can tell us about the
literary value of various parts of Emily Brontë's work, but
rather in what they can tell us about the *cultural context* in
which the poems were written and have been read. As
Margaret Homans has suggested, Emily Brontë's work is
as interesting for its failures as for its successes, because
it demonstrates 'the immensity of the difficulties to be
confronted by any woman poet'.(10)

Gender may well have played an important part in
the construction of the Gondal framework. Ideas about
gender have certainly played a key role in the critical
debate about Gondal. On the whole, the anti-Gondalians
see Emily Brontë's poetry in relation to the dominant – that
is to say, patriarchal – literary tradition, and they emphasise
and value those aspects of the poet's work which fit most
coherently into this tradition. Thus Derek Stanford, one

of the most radical of the anti-Gondalians, thinks that
Emily Brontë's most successful poems are those which
most thoroughly assimilate and internalise the dominant
masculine tradition. What Stanford proclaims as Emily
Brontë's own distinctive voice reads in his description
more like a virtuoso feat of ventriloquism.

> [I]n Emily's best poems – her half-dozen pieces which
> must be classed as major poems of the English lan-
> guage . . . she speaks in so *assimilated* a style that any
> foreign influences seem fused together in it, presenting
> an accent, a rhythm, thought and diction peculiarly and
> personally her own. (150, my emphasis)

For others Gondal represents a self-indulgent fantasy, an
escape, and a symptom of 'childhood's enduring hold on
adult Victorian women' (Hewish, 76).

It is, however, possible to take an alternative view of
Emily Brontë's poetry, which places Gondal at its centre.
This view tends to be held by those who seek to understand
the distinctiveness of Emily Brontë's voice; who attempt to
investigate rather than simply report 'childhood's enduring
hold on adult Victorian women'; who ask serious questions
about the nature and significance of the Gondal world, about
why Emily Brontë needed Gondal and how she used it; who
see this elaborate creation of a complex private world as a
positive construction rather than as a 'cardboard sublime'
(Stanford, 128), a merely negative retreat from the harsh
realities of everyday life.

Fanny Ratchford's claim that Gondal is 'a tightly knit
epic of the free, wild, grotesque world of imagination
which nourished Emily's creative genius and brought it to
its fruitage',[8] has been taken up enthusiastically, if rather
loosely, by recent feminist critics. Ratchford was one of
the earliest, and certainly one of the staunchest, of the
proponents of the view that Emily Brontë's poems as they

are known to twentieth-century readers are the remnant of a larger work in verse and prose, the lost epic of Gondal. In her preface to C.W. Hatfield's edition of *The Complete Poems of Emily Jane Brontë*, Ratchford attempted to relate the circumstances of Gondal's creation, to reconstruct the development of the Gondal story, and to arrange the poems 'in their natural order as an epic'.

> When Charlotte . . . went away to school at Roe Head early in 1831, Emily, refusing to accept her brother Branwell as Charlotte's successor, began a play of her own with her younger sister Anne. Its setting was Gondal, an island in the North Pacific, a land of lakes, mountains and rocky shorelines, with a climate much like Emily's native Yorkshire. Its people were a strong, passionate freedom-loving race, highly imaginative and intensely patriotic. Politically, Gondal was a confederacy of provinces or kingdoms, each governed by an hereditary ruling family. Between the House of Brenzaida, in the Kingdom of Angora, and the House of Exina existed a deadly rivalry which gave direction to the developing play. (H, p.14)

In her later work, *Gondal's Queen*, Ratchford attempted to reconstruct the connecting narrative, and to flesh out the characters and events of the epic. According to this reconstruction the epic's chief character is Augusta Geraldine Almeda or A.G.A., sometimes known as Rosina, Princess of Alcona,

> Worshiped [sic] of all men who came under her charms, she brought tragedy to those upon whom her amorous light shone – death in battle to Lord Elbe; exile and death to Amadeus; exile and suicide to Lord Alfred; imprisonment, madness, and suicide to Fernando; assassination to Julius. (*Gondal's Queen*, 41)

Ratchford's 'Argument' suggests that her taste for melodrama is quite equal to Emily Brontë's own. Moreover, despite her efforts, the existence of a lost epic of Gondal and its exact nature, must remain a matter of speculation. However, as long as we read it sceptically and provisionally, Ratchford's attempted reconstruction of the Gondal saga provides a context for the poems and helps us to find our bearings amidst the confusion and incompleteness of the Gondal maze.

Whether or not there was a large and unified Gondal narrative, the existence of the Gondal characters and their adventures cannot be denied. Simply to dismiss the Gondal dimension is to ignore the central role that Gondal played in Emily Brontë's imaginative life. Why did Emily Brontë devote herself to such a project, and what does her commitment to Gondal tell us about the writer and her art? Nina Auerbach's observation that 'Gondal was the secret room in Emily Brontë's imagination',[9] provides an important clue to Gondal's significance.

Emily Brontë wrote her poems secretly, and did not, apparently, intend them for publication. Like her life, her poems have been hidden from history. She published only twenty one poems in her lifetime, although a further eighteen appeared in the 1850 edition of *Wuthering Heights and Agnes Grey*, and a few others subsequently surfaced in periodicals. C.W. Hatfield's *Complete Poems* in 1941 brought some 193 poems and fragments into the public domain, but even so, Emily Brontë's work remains very private, and in the absence of the Gondal story many of the poems withhold their meanings. The Gondal locations and stories themselves constitute a private history and geography, created and shared only by Emily and Anne Brontë. Indeed Anne's Birthday Paper of 1845 suggests that Emily's poems were concealed even from her collaborator.

Emily is engaged in writing the emperor Julius's life. She has read some of it, and I want very much to hear

the rest. She is writing some poetry too, I wonder what
it is about. (LL II, 52)

Although the Gondal characters and situations owe
much to Byron and something to the ballad tradition,
the Gondal world remains distinctively Emily Brontë's
own creation. In this self-enclosed, self-contained, and
self-generated world, Emily Brontë created a dramatic
alternative to both the world in which she lived, and the
world whose literary tradition and history she had only
partially inherited. It is as though in creating the history
and geography of Gondal, its heroes and villains, its battles
and political intrigues, the banishments or self-exile of its
characters, Emily Brontë was supplementing the 'shreds and
patches of feeble literature and false history'[10] which most
young women usually received at this time. The military
insurrections, intrigues, and imperial ambitions that form
the centre of the Gondal narrative might be seen as Emily
Brontë's rewriting and mythologising of recent European
history. But most importantly, as J. Hillis Miller has noted,
Gondal provides an alternative 'myth kitty' to that which
informs the dominant literary tradition.

> The Gondal events did not become, like historical
> happenings part of a vanished past after they had
> occurred. They functioned for Emily Brontë just as
> religious myths functioned for the Greek poets . . .
> Transformed into a collection of eternal events, they
> were happening over and over again all the time, always
> there to be returned to and recreated in poetry.[11]

In the absence of poetic 'grandmothers', and largely
excluded from the dominant male literary tradition, Emily
Brontë re-wrote or re-invented a mythological tradition.
Emily Brontë is thus doubly an author. She first authors
the world which subsequently becomes the subject of,

and provides the mythological structure for, the poems that she authors. Looked at in this light, Emily Brontë's commitment to the private Gondal world appears to be positively empowering rather than a self-indulgent escape. Gondal provides the author with a means of transcending the trap of female passivity so inhibiting to the woman writer, particularly the would-be lyric poet, who must overcome her 'culturally conditioned timidity about self-dramatization, her dread of the patriarchal authority of art, her anxiety about the impropriety of female invention' (Gilbert and Gubar (a), 50).

Although this timidity and anxiety might be said to inhibit all forms of female creativity in the nineteenth century, it can be argued that it was more inimical to poetry than to the novel. The characteristic posture of the narrator of the nineteenth-century novel as a reporter, observer, and sympathetic mediator between the reader and the fictional world was relatively easily accommodated to the traditional view of woman's abilities. On the other hand, the voice of a lyric poem, even when it involves a persona or a mask, is usually 'the utterance of a strong and assertive "I"' (Gilbert and Gubar (b), xxii). Such assertiveness clearly sits uneasily with dominant nineteenth-century views of the feminine. The woman poet must thus transform herself from the socially and culturally conditioned role of sympathetic and patient observer into an active singer and declaimer,

> assertive, authoritative, radiant with powerful feelings while at the same time absorbed in her own consciousness – and hence, by definition, profoundly "unwomanly" even freakish. (Gilbert and Gubar (b), xxii)

In Gondal Emily Brontë created a series of dramatic situations, personae, and masks by means of which she could escape some of the restrictions of the culturally conditioned female voice: heroic warriors calling their troops to battle, adventurers wandering the high seas, and, most interesting of all, proud, powerful and assertive women such as Angelica and A.G.A., who are often portrayed through the perspective of their desperate and spurned lovers whom they inspire to commit terrible deeds.

It is perhaps not surprising that some male critics should have found this image of the female rather threatening. C. Day Lewis, for example, was thrown into a frenzy of adjectives by Gondal's heroine Augusta, 'that *femme fatale* – proud, ruthless, impatient, dominating, essentially destructive'.[12] In his effort to explain away Brontë's powerful women Day Lewis read them symptomatically, appealing to an imaginary psychologist who might see in them 'an image of Emily's own conflict, the conflict of a woman who in phantasy imprisons or destroys men because she cannot *be* a man' (Brontë Society Transactions, 67, 97). Certainly we might agree with the view that Emily Brontë's powerful women are images of her own conflict, but we might more usefully see the source of that conflict not in her supposed dissatisfaction with her sex, but in her difficulty in reconciling a particular and socially constructed notion of the female gender with her own sense of selfhood. Rather than viewing Brontë's powerful women as neurotic symptoms, more or less passive reflections of their author's disturbed psyche, we might instead focus on the way in which they both embody and investigate conflict, and negotiate the prevailing limiting definitions of the feminine.

Emily Brontë's powerful women offer female versions of the Romantic exile, that outcast, outlawed, or otherwise isolated figure, the lonely bearer of the truth who rejects or rebels against the society from which he has been exiled. Ultimately, however, the assertiveness of Brontë's powerful women is problematic, and is accompanied by a sense of isolation which is shared by many of her dramatic voices in both the Gondal and the non-Gondal poems. Isolated from humanity at large, by virtue of their distinctive or special nature, exiled from their community by love, treachery, or the accidents of history, these speakers perhaps dramatise Brontë's sense of her own freakishness and exceptionality.

4 Death Dreams and Prison Songs

In her Gondal verses Emily Brontë invents personae and develops situations which enable her to return repeatedly to the same preoccupations. The first poem in the Gondal Notebook, 'There shines the moon at noon of night' (H 9, 33) introduces many of her recurring concerns. Like so many of Emily Brontë's poems these lines have a night-time setting; the darkness of the night and the isolation of the setting mirrors the isolation of the speaker (A.G.A.), while the moon, 'Vision of glory-Dream of light!', acts as an image of (and perhaps a stimulus for) an imaginative transcendence of the darkness, isolation, exile and death which figure so prominently in Emily Brontë's verse. A.G.A. meditates on her past life and her lost lover, Elbe, reflecting on the various states of exile she has experienced; from her homeland; from her lover, who has met a bloody death; from the site of his grave, to which after many years her 'weary feet return at last'. She is exiled too from her former self, through the necessities of time and change.

> And Earth's the same but oh to see
> How wildly Time has altered me!
> Am I the being who long ago
> Sat watching by that water side,

'There shines the moon' is also about forgetfulness and memory, about what is lost through time and what persists. A.G.A.'s memories of Elbe's death add another layer both to these themes and to the twin themes of alienation and exile. In recalling Elbe's death A.G.A. does not simply tell its story, but rather appropriates his dying consciousness and makes it sing a song which prefigures and echoes her own song in the poem's dramatic present. Emily Brontë repeatedly makes use of this layering effect (particularly in the Gondal poems) to give a double focus, to tell the same story twice, to displace the lyric intensities. It is a technique whose possibilities she was to explore further in *Wuthering Heights*.

Imprisonment and exile, intense passions and bloody deaths are of course the stuff of which Gondal is made, but even in the early and far from accomplished poem from which I have just quoted, Emily Brontë explores as well as exploits the melodramatic possibilities of the situations she creates. Almost all the Gondal situations involve matters of life and death, and life is constantly viewed through the perspective of death. This preoccupation with death is one which Emily Brontë shares with Victorian culture in general. She lived and wrote in what Patsy Stoneman has described as a 'death-orientated society' in which 'the predominant evangelical religion saw life as a vale of tears, a valley of affliction, a sore preparation for the life to come.' This shared preoccupation with death generated a common imagery of bondage and restraint, as in the following Wesleyan hymn.

> Rejoice for a brother deceased,
> Our loss is his infinite gain;
> A soul out of prison released
> And freed from its bodily chain.[1]

We can immediately recognise in these lines some of the dominant imagery of Emily Brontë's verse. 'A.S. TO G.S. . . . ' is just one of numerous examples of poems which fit neatly into the hymn's conceptual frame.

I do not weep, I would not weep;
Our Mother needs no tears;
Dry thine eyes too, 'tis vain to keep
This causeless grief for years.
. . .
Remember still she is not dead,
she sees us Gerald, now,
Laid where her angel spirit fled
'Mid heath and frozen snow.
(H 152, 172-3)

Emily Brontë's own particular obsession with death, however, moves beyond the perspectives and imagery of evangelical religion as she explores death as a desired alternative to specific limitations, and as a means of transcending or reconciling life's discontinuities and contradictions. Moreover, while some poems, or parts of poems, acknowledge (methodistically) that it is 'vain to keep/This causeless grief for years', in others the images and concepts owe as much to Romanticism as to Methodism. In such poems Brontë repeatedly explores the ironies and complexities of the experience of loss and grief. Both of these states are represented in terms of images of exile and alienation. Death itself is represented as a condition of permanent exile, but its very permanence is also an escape from life's constant change.

The Gondal poems repeatedly return to the theme of mutability as the condition of life in nature and in time. All things in nature constantly grow, change and develop, but they also decay and die. Similarly, the poems focus on the mutability of human relationships, which are also subject to change and development, denial and betrayal. For example, 'Come, walk with me' (H 172, 203–4) uses images of a partially and provisionally recuperative nature to expose the inconstancy of human relationships.

> "Is human love so true?
> Can Friendship's flower droop on for years
> And then revive anew?
> No; though the soil be wet with tears,
> How fair so'er it grew;
> The vital sap once perishèd
> Will never flow again;
> And surer than that dwelling dread,
> The narrow dungeon of the dead,
> Time parts the hearts of men."

A number of the Gondal poems oppose the constancy of death to life's inconstancy. For example, 'In the earth, the earth thou shalt be laid' (H 163, 190) explicitly represents death as a means of escaping the inconstancy of mortal affection. In this poem, paradoxically, life is seen as cold and destructive while the cold grave becomes the seed-bed which nurtures a constant memory.

> But cold, cold in that resting place,
> Shut out from Joy and Liberty,
> And all who loved thy living face
> Will shrink from its gloom and thee.
>
> "Not so: *here* the world is chill,
> And sworn friends fall from me;
> But *there*, they'll own me still
> And prize my memory."
>
> Farewell, then, all that love,
> All that deep sympathy:
> Sleep on; heaven laughs above.
> Earth never misses thee.

The fragile complexities of memory are most perhaps delicately explored in one of Brontë's best known poems,

'Cold in the earth' (H 182, 222). This poem acknowledges
the potentially treacherous nature of memory's erosion by
time while simultaneously celebrating time and change.

> Cold in the earth, and the deep snow piled above thee!
> Far, far removed, cold in the dreary grave!
> Have I forgot, my Only Love, to love thee,
> Severed at last by Time's all-wearing wave?
>
> Now, when alone, do my thoughts no longer hover
> Over the mountains on Angora's shore;
> Resting their wings where heath and fern-leaves cover
> That noble heart for ever, ever more?
>
> Cold in the earth, and fifteen wild Decembers
> From those brown hills have melted into spring –
> Faithful indeed is the spirit that remembers
> After such years of change and suffering!

The poised ambiguity of this last exclamation, which
expresses both wonderment and surprise, is echoed in the
way the rest of the poem balances memory and forgetfulness, the persistence of love (that is, its permanence) and
the persistence of life which involves constant change.

If time is the destroyer of memory and of love, then
memory is potentially the destroyer of life and the source
of a seductively 'rapturous pain' whose 'divinest anguish'
pulls the speaker towards death and the tomb. Ultimately
'Cold in the earth' eschews the comforts of either Christian
affirmation – death as life eternal, life triumphant – or
surrender to Romantic intensities of feeling, offering
instead a tentative reconciliation to a life of 'change and
suffering'. However, the poem remains delicately poised,
and the fragility of its sense of acceptance is underlined
by its movement into the present tense in the final stanza
which ends, significantly, not with affirmation but with a
question,

And even yet I dare not let it languish,
Dare not indulge in Memory's rapturous pain;
Once drinking deep of that divinest anguish,
How could I seek the empty world again?

Through the persona of Rosina Alcona Emily Brontë
rehearses and explores a minimally humanist acceptance
of a life of chance, choice and change grounded in human
love. She refuses the escape route offered by death at the
same time that she acknowledges, and even flirts with, its
powerful attractions. In this poem at least, death is not
embraced as a means of transcending the emotional and
physical sufferings of mortal life.

Emily Brontë continually returned to the conventional
imagery of bondage, restraint and release through which
the Wesleyan hymn (quoted earlier) celebrates death as the
release of the soul into life eternal. However, her poems
often use the imagery of the body as the soul's prison,
and death as its liberator in order to explore and question
it. While one poem can celebrate the broadly Christian
paradox that the 'eternal midnight' of the 'undergloom' is
a glorious escape from 'Earth's dungeon tomb' (H, 186),
others explore the irony that death, the liberator, 'releases'
the human body into the prison of the grave, that 'narrow
dungeon of the dead' (H, p.204) by which we are 'Shut out
from Joy and Liberty' (H, p.190).

Interestingly, the paradoxes and ironies in Brontë's
treatment of this topic are articulated in poems whose
style and structure are characteristic of her work as a
whole. For example, 'Where beams the sun the brightest'
(H 158, 186), 'Come, walk with me' (H 173, 203–4), and
'In the earth, the earth, thou shalt be laid (H 163, 190)
all indulge in extreme states of feeling and, at the same
time, observe and place those feelings. This double focus
is accompanied not only by a typically Brontëan dualism on
the subject of the competing pains and pleasures of life and

death, but also by a structural duality. Each of these poems, like so much of Brontë's work, proceeds by a series of ironic shifts and displacements, and expresses its tensions and conflicts in the form of either a monologue addressed to an unspecified 'Thou' ('Where beams the sun'), or a dialogue or debate between two (again unspecified) voices, one of which rehearses the natural vitality of the sensuous mortal world and its negation in death, while the other proclaims the glorious changelessness of death.

Shades of the prison house

It is not difficult to see why a nineteenth-century woman so fiercely concerned with liberty should see prisons and tombs on every side. However, C. Day Lewis, writing in 1957, saw the matter differently.

> Why all the fuss? She wanted liberty. Well didn't she have it? A reasonably satisfactory home-life, a most satisfactory dream-life – why then all this beating of wings? What was this cage, invisible to us, which she felt herself to be confined in? (Brontë Society Transactions, 67, 94)

To which one can only answer that it is perfectly reasonable for a woman (or anyone) to desire more in life than a reasonably satisfactory home-life. Indeed it was essential to most Romantic theories of the poet that he (sic) should aspire beyond the restrictions of domestic and social norms. One might answer too that it is precisely the false consolations of a 'satisfactory dream-life' which Emily Brontë's poems repeatedly dramatise and analyse, even if they do not always avoid them. Without 'all the fuss' there would probably have been no poems.

If many of the Gondal poems view death through images of imprisonment, many others are concerned with the death in life that is imprisonment. 'Gleneden's Dream', 'Written in the Gaaldine Prison Caves to A.G.A.', 'From a Dungeon Wall in the Southern College', 'M.A. Written On The Dungeon Wall – N.C.' and 'Julian M. and A.G. Rochelle', all rehearse the theme of a living death which is vividly conveyed in F. De Samara's outburst against the captors who 'spare my life, to kill my mind'. (H, p.139) In all of these poems the wind, sun and moon act as reminders of the natural world, a world of constant change beyond the static existence inside the walls of the damp, dark dungeons which so closely resemble the tomb. Death becomes a desired means of escape, the means of transcending the now heightened sufferings and bondage of mortal life. However, interestingly, some of the prison poems also suggest alternative means of transcendence: in memory, imagination, and vision. Gleneden, for example, is saved from 'Death and Desolation' by dreams of 'Heaven, descending in a vision', which 'Taught my soul to do and bear'. (H, 73) Her almost obsessive concern with dramatising and exploring visionary states suggests that vision and imagination performed a similarly saving function for Emily Brontë. This is seen at its least fraught and complex in 'I'm happiest when most away' (H 44, 63) in which the soul exalts in its transcendence of mortal limits, and its capacity to merge oceanically with the 'light' of the night-time world. Here Brontë's penchant for extreme regularity of rhyme and rhythm almost suggests that the recurring visionary moment articulated in the poem is an unexceptional, everyday occurrence.

Perhaps the most interesting of the prison poems is 'Julian M. and A.G. Rochelle', usually printed, as it was in 1846, as 'The Prisoner: A Fragment', with the Gondal elements omitted. The poem depicts a pathetic and wasting female prisoner, A.G. Rochelle (A.G.A.) and two male captors – a surly prison guard, and the narrator Julian M. Like the other prison poems it dwells on the utter desolation of the captive who compares her dungeon to a 'living grave' (H, 238), which she wishes to exchange for a real one,

> "Not buried under earth but in the open sky;
> By ball or speedy knife or headsman's skilful blow –
> A quick, and welcome pang instead of lingering woe!"

The most remarkable section of the poem is undoubtedly the lyric passage in which A.G. Rochelle describes the recurring visionary experience which saves her from 'gloom and desolate despair'.

> "A messenger of Hope, comes every night to me,
> And offers, for short life, eternal liberty.
> He comes with western winds, with evening's wandering
>   airs,
> With that clear dusk of heaven that brings the thickest stars;
> Winds take a pensive tone, and stars a tender fire,
> And visions rise and change which kill me with desire –

The visionary visitant is, in a sense, an image of death or prefigures death, but is not death itself. Like death the 'messenger of Hope' affords A.G. Rochelle a means of transcending the constraints of her imprisonment in the dungeon and in mortal, physical life. The messenger heralds an intense, visionary experience which takes the prisoner out of her body into the disembodied realms of the imagination, the 'Invisible', the 'Unseen', where 'outward sense' is replaced by the 'inward essence'. In the context of the poem's narrative development (largely unavailable to readers of the de-Gondalised 'Fragment' version), this intense imaginative experience not only raises A.G. Rochelle above the restrictions of her physical conditions, but also reconciles her to her bondage: her vision becomes the reality and the dungeon an illusion. Thus, when Julian responds to her pathos by breaking her bonds she remains in her cell, apparently accepting willingly the bondage against which she had formerly chafed.

Although the visionary experience represented in this poem is given a carefully created dramatic context, it is tempting to see Emily Brontë's own experience in A.G. Rochelle's imaginative transcendence of her imprisoned state. Both author and persona share a restricted life: A.G. Rochelle is bound by the walls of her prison, Emily Brontë by the limitations of the circumstances of her life as the daughter of a nineteenth-century clergyman in a remote parish in the north of England. Both author and character achieve the freedom they desire by withdrawing from the world into a state of imaginative or mystical possession which gives them the power of transcending or, alternatively, becoming reconciled to those restrictions.

Fleeing the Prison: Visionary Visitants and the Liberation of the Imagination

Like so many of the Gondal poems which dramatise the literal imprisonment of their protagonists, 'Julian M. and A.G. Rochelle' suggests that true liberty lies in a liberation of the imagination through a visionary experience analogous to the emancipation of the soul by physical death. This liberating visionary experience is also a central concern of many of the non-Gondal poems. In these poems, as in some of the Gondal verses, the visionary experience and call to liberty come from a visionary visitant, heralded by the 'western winds', who brings the power of transcendence which will liberate the captive spirit.

The mental landscape of visionary visitation is sketched out in two early poems, 'The night is darkening round me' and 'I'll come when thou art saddest', both dated November 1836. In the first poem the 'darkening' night and 'The wild winds' conspire to draw the resisting speaker away from

consciousness and mortal life. The second, uncharacteristi-
cally written from the point of view of the visionary visitant,
a creature of 'evening's chilly gloom', also promises to 'bear
thy soul away'. The language of visitation and possession is
developed and elaborated in many of the poems transcribed
into the untitled notebook in 1844. Indeed, one critic has
gone so far as to suggest that in selecting and grouping the
poems concerned with vision and imaginative possession
Emily Brontë was 'self-consciously developing a myth of
the imagination' (Homans, 109). Emily Brontë's visionary
visitant is sometimes shade, sometimes muse; a ghostly
figure from the regions of death, or the bringer of vision
and imagination. As always in Emily Brontë's poems death
and vision are closely related as means of transcendence.

This habitual correlation of death and vision as images
of transcendence might be seen as a consequence of the
female poet's problematic relationship to the Romantic
myth of transcendence, and indeed to the whole Romantic
discourse of poetry. The woman poet is progressively
excluded from this discourse, which not only defines
the poet as 'a man speaking to men' (Wordsworth,
'Preface' to *Lyrical Ballads*), but also accords to this
male speaker the status of the universal subject, the
transcendent representative of the whole of humanity.
The authority of experience in which this transcendent
Romantic subjectivity is grounded, is thus the authority of
male experience. Emily Brontë's preoccupation with death,
and with visionary visitants may perhaps be seen as attempts
to negotiate the problems posed for the woman poet by these
definitions and exclusions. Some of her poems, or some
aspects of those poems, seem to explore the idea that, for
the female poet, Romantic transcendence is achieved (if at
all) not through the intensification of (male) subjectivity,
but by the annihilation of the female self, either in death
or by yielding to a source of vision outside the self.[2]

The correlation of death and vision as images of

transcendence is clearly shown in a group of poems from 1840, 'Far, far away is mirth withdrawn', 'I'll not weep that thou art going to leave me', and 'If grief for grief can touch thee'. In each of these poems the visionary presence is a shade, external to the speaker and summoned up to comfort her, or to take her away from a burdensome and, to use an habitual Brontëan term, 'dreary' existence. As in so much of Brontë's work the self-dramatising and posturing of these poems teeters on the brink of a potentially bathetic melodrama. As, for example, in the histrionic cries to the 'Deserted one!', whose 'corpse lies cold,/And mingled with a foreign mould', with its tears which

> . . .deluge my heart like the rain
> On cursed Gomorrah's howling plain

('Far, far away', H 134, 140). Only the sharp recoil into the dramatic present and the waking world rescues this poem.

> "What have I dreamt? He lies asleep
> With whom my heart would vainly weep:
> *He* rests, and *I* endure the woe
> That left his spirit long ago.

In another poem in this group – 'It is too late to call thee now' – the shade is associated with an intense possession which belongs to a world of dream and vision, and the desire for escape is replaced by a desire to merge with the visiting spirit which begins to resemble a muse rather than death's lure:

> Yet, ever in my grateful breast,
> Thy darling shade shall cherished be.
> (H 135, 142)

The visitant becomes more muselike, and is further inter-
nalised and integrated with the speaker's inner life in a later
group of poems (dated 1844) which develops into a sort of
debate about the sources of vision and imagination. For
example, although 'My Comforter' addresses an external
spirit with the familiar request to 'Calm this resentful mood',
the spirit thus addressed performs its task by drawing upon
and drawing out the speaker's own inner resources. Here
the sources of vision seem to be located within the self and
the speech of the visitant is an echo of the lyric 'I'.

> Well hast thou spoken – and yet not taught
> A feeling strange or new;
> Thou hast but roused a latent thought,
> A cloud-closed beam of sunshine brought
> To gleam in open view.
>
> (H 168, 196)

'To Imagination' also represents the sources of vision
as simultaneously within and without. This later poem is
also addressed to an external and possibly delusive source
of solace; a 'benignant power' but also an untrustworthy
'phantom bliss'. Like 'My Comforter', the external spirit
of 'To Imagination' also inhabits the speaker's inner world,
and the state of imaginative possession which results from
this merging is equated with liberty:

> So hopeless is the world without,
> The world within I doubly prize;
> Thy world where guile and hate and doubt
> And cold suspicion never rise;
> Where thou and I and Liberty
> Have undisputed sovereignty

The 'benignant power' liberates through its capacity to
transcend 'nature's sad reality', 'the suffering heart' and

the 'Truth' that tramples down 'The flowers of Fancy', and to bring together real and fantasy worlds:

> But thou art ever there to bring
> The hovering visions back and breathe
> New glories o'er the blighted spring
> And call a lovelier life from death,
> And whisper with a voice divine
> Of real worlds as bright as thine.
>
> (H 174, 205-6)

In contrast, the 'radiant angel' of 'O thy bright eyes must answer now', is summoned not as a 'comforter', nor a 'solacer of human cares', but as an alternative voice which must defend the speaker's choice of visions and 'a strange road', as opposed to 'Stern Reason' and 'The common paths that others run'. Vision and imagination are figured now not as providing consolation for the pains of the real world, nor a means of reconciling real and dream worlds, but rather as an alternative order of being, freakish but necessary. The speaker's relationship to the visiting angel is also significantly different from the relationships in 'My Comforter' and 'To Imagination'. In 'O thy bright eyes' the speaker is simultaneously *possessor* and *possessed*, and the 'God of Visions' is simultaneously 'My slave, my comrade, and my King!' Significantly the superiority of the 'God of Visions', and his potential 'mastery' of the speaker lies in the presumed authority of his speech. The poem begins and ends with the speaker's plea for the God of Visions to *speak for her*, and thus cedes the power of speech to an authoritative voice outside the self, suggesting once again the problem (discussed in detail by Margaret Homans) that the nineteenth-century female poet experienced in finding and trusting to the power of her own voice.

In many of her poems addressed to visionary visitants

Emily Brontë appears to reverse the convention by which
male poets invoke a female muse. However, more than a
simple reversal of conventions is involved, since in many of
these poems the masculine, or grammatically ungendered,
muse is not simply invoked, but rather becomes the subject
of the poem. Such poems both articulate the struggle against
the restriction experienced by the woman poet, and are
about the struggle to articulate.

This is seen particularly clearly in a number of poems
which directly address the wind or invoke it as muse. Some
of these poems repeat the pattern of the visitant poems. For
example, in the following three poems the wind is seen by
turns as a shade which lures the speaker toward easeful
death, a voice from another realm which merges with the
speaker, and a presence which offers the speaker a language
and song which is richer than her own. In 'The Night-Wind'
the wind is heard as a seductive voice of song wooing the
speaker away from life to the shadowy regions of death.

> "O come," it sighed so sweetly
> "I'll win thee 'gainst thy will.
>
> . . .
>
> "Have I not loved thee long?
> As long as thou hast loved the night
> Whose silence wakes my song.
>
> (H 140, 147)

The association with death is also present in 'Aye, there it
is! It wakes tonight', in which death is part of a gloriously
liberating transcendence, as the wind awakens 'sweet
thoughts that will not die', makes 'wild fancy' play, and
rekindles 'feeling's fires'. This poem is typical of Brontë's
lyric art in its movement through a series of progressively
intensified lyric moments. In this case these lyric moments
are registered in the stanzaic pattern: each stanza represents
a different aspect and successive phase of the process by

which the subjectivity of the speaker becomes progressively intensified through its interaction with the natural world. The poem builds towards a climactic vision of merging, as the 'thou' merges with the wind and is thus liberated from the limitations of mortal existence in a prefiguration of death.

> And thou art now a spirit pouring
> Thy presence into all –
> . . .
>
> A universal influence
> From thine own influence free;
> A principle of life, intense
> Lost to mortality.
>
> Thus truly when that breast is cold
> Thy prisoned soul shall rise,
> The dungeon mingle with the mould –
> The captive with the skies.
>
> (H 148, 165)

'Loud without the wind was roaring' also represents the wind as the liberator of the spirit that 'longed . . . burned to be free!', but here the wind more closely approximates the visionary visitant as muse, as it awakens in the speaker's memory or unconscious the 'Wild words of an ancient song,/Undefined, without a name' (H 91, 90). The 'ancient song' is one of those forgotten songs, referred to by Christina Rossetti, which link the poem's speaking subject to a forgotten continuity and awaken a Romantic longing. The 'ancient song' is simultaneously a reminder and a transcendence of an exile which is both spatial – 'in exile afar,/On the brow of a lonely hill kneeling' – and temporal – an exile from

> The time when nor labour nor dreaming
> Broke the sleep of the happy and free.

The 'ancient song' which the wind activates is also a song of nature, the alternative source of vision in Emily Brontë's myth of the imagination. 'Loud without' celebrates the process by which a lost harmony with nature can be recovered through vision, and lyric intensities. The song of nature transforms the gloom of 'cloudy November' through its recovery of the 'music of May'. However, while the central, celebratory stanzas demonstrate the power of poetic language to perform such an act of recovery, at the same time (as so often in Emily Brontë's verse) this poem, with its yearning cry 'What language can utter the feeling', also engages with the problem of the adequacy of its own language.

The 'ancient song' of 'Loud without' is echoed by the 'strange minstrelsy' of the later 'A Day Dream' (H 170, 198–200). Here the speaker, a typical Brontëan figure, represents herself as a discordant element among nature's 'wedding guests' at 'the marriage-time of May/With her young lover June'. The speaker's alienation from nature is expressed in the contending visions produced by the self-communing of the fragments of her divided self.

> So, resting on a healthy bank,
> I took my heart to me;
> And we together sadly sank
> Into a reverie.

The reverie, articulated in the ensuing stanzas, comprises a series of visions which see beyond present realities, and apparently see through the surfaces of the natural world, producing an anti-Romantic version of the seasonal cycle in which nature is destructive rather than recuperative.

> We thought, "When winter comes again,
> Where will these bright things be?
> All vanished like a vision vain,
> An unreal mockery!

"The birds that now so blithely sing,
Through deserts frozen dry,
Poor spectres of the perished Spring
In famished troops will fly.

"And why should we be glad at all?
The leaf is hardly green,
Before a token of the fall
Is on its surface seen."

This cynical self-communing is, however, transfigured by a vision of futurity, 'full of sparks divine', which employs and, simultaneously, transforms the conventional Christian imagery of the 'universal joy' of the 'endless rest,/And everlasting day' beyond the 'veil' of mortal life. As in so many of Brontë's poems the sources of this vision are partly outside the self and clearly owe something to Christian mysticism, but the visions are also, in part, self-generated: the 'little glittering spirits' which 'sang/Or *seemed* to sing to me' (my emphasis), are also the 'fond creations' of 'Fancy'. This double awareness is maintained throughout the poem's superficially triumphant concluding stanzas. The lyric intensities imply and, indeed, solicit a commitment to a Romantic vision which is, however, subtly undermined (although not dispelled) by the qualifying comment and the return to the daylight, waking world.

The music ceased – the noonday Dream
Like dream of night withdrew
But Fancy still will sometimes deem
Her fond creation true.

A number of poems written at the same time as 'Loud without', develop a Wordsworthian sense of nature as a source of vision. 'A little while, a little while', for example, explicitly sees Nature as a spiritual resource which can transport 'my harassed heart' beyond 'my dungeon bars' of 'weary care'. However, nature is ultimately just as problematic a source of imaginative vision as is the self in the poems discussed earlier, and for similar reasons. In the Romantic, particularly the Wordsworthian discourse of poetry, nature is feminine and women are subsumed into nature as in Wordsworth's Lucy poems. As Margaret Homans has pointed out, this identification of nature with the female clearly creates problems for a woman who seeks to write within a Romantic tradition which constructs her as the bearer rather than the maker of meanings.

Like the earlier visionary visitants nature too is seen as potentially threatening to overcome or 'master' the speaker. This sense of threat is felt particularly strongly in 'Shall earth no more inspire thee', in which the wind speaks as a God or spirit of nature asserting his 'mighty sway' and 'magic power' in an effort to recall his 'wayward Votary'. Moreover, if the wind in Emily Brontë's poems is a bringer of vision and song, it is also a reminder of self-division and death, as in 'The wind I hear it sighing', where it induces a painful awareness of the discontinuities and contradictions of the speaker's present and former selves. The desire for self-integrity, for a unified sense of the self, together with a simultaneous awareness and fear of the self's diffusion and fragmentation, lies at the heart of both the Gondal and the non-Gondal poetry. Brontë's poems constantly seek ways of holding the self together, but they achieve this self-unity only in brief moments of stasis as in the uncharacteristic twilight calm of 'All day I've toiled . . . '

> All day I've toiled, but not with pain,
> In learning's golden mine;
> And now at eventide again
> The moonbeams softly shine
> . . .

> O may I never lose the peace
> That lulls me gently now,
>   . . .
> True to myself, and true to all,
> May I be healthful still,
> And turn away from passion's call,
> And curb my own wild will.
>
> (H 10, 35)

Elsewhere this elusive self-unity can only be nostalgically recalled as a momentary pre-linguistic state.

> And thoughts in my soul were gushing,
> And my heart bowed beneath their power;
> And tears within my eyes were rushing
> Because I could not speak the feeling,
> The solemn joy around me stealing
> In that divine, untroubled hour.
>
> (H 27, 48)

Here the irregular syllabics (a mixture of eight and nine syllable lines) interrupt that rhythmic fluency which is a notable (and some would argue regrettable and limiting) feature of Brontë's verse, and announce the disharmonies and fragmentation which almost invariably result when her vision seeks articulation in language.

> "Dreams have encircled me," I said,
> "From careless childhood's sunny time;
> Visions by ardent fancy fed
> Since life was in its morning prime."
>
> But now, when I had hoped to sing,
> My fingers strike a tuneless string;
> And still the burden of the strain
> Is "Strive no more; 'tis all in vain."

It is, perhaps, this tension between vision, a curiously unselfconscious state of intensified subjectivity, and a self-conscious articulation in language, which lies at the heart of the conflicts and contradictions from which Emily Brontë's poems are constructed.

Throughout Emily Brontë's poetry division, contradiction, discontinuity, alienation, isolation, and exile are dramatised in dialogues, debates, interior monologues, or intense lyric outpourings. On the other hand, nature in its cyclic continuity is offered as a source of harmony, and death is figured as the resolver of all contradictions, the harmoniser of discontinuity, and a means of transcendence that will liberate the imprisoned spirit. At first glance this would seem to be a strange confounding of Romanticism and Victorian evangelicalism, but I would suggest that this curious convergence has the effect of displacing and questioning both Romantic theories of the fragmentation of the self and the healing powers of nature, and the evangelical view of death as the release from a vale of tears into a transcendent heaven. This displacement and questioning becomes a focus for the articulation of Emily Brontë's discontents, and her questioning of social and religious norms.

This process is clearly visible in two of her most widely anthologised poems, which present death as a fusion of self and nature, rather than as an escape from a mortal life in the natural world. 'I see around me tombstones grey' eschews the consoling comforts of Heaven for a stark acceptance of 'Time and Death and Mortal pain' which is expressed as a fervent commitment to 'mother' earth. The transcendence of heaven is rejected in favour of a fusion with the earth in death.

> We would not leave our native home
> For *any* world beyond the Tomb.
> No – rather on thy kindly breast

Let us be laid in lasting rest;
Or waken but to share with thee
A mutual immortality.

(H 149, 167)

While this poem begins by opposing Heaven and Earth, it
ends by reconciling them, at least in language, by making
a heaven of earth. 'Death that struck While I was most
confiding', on the other hand, begins by opposing 'Time's
withered branch' and the 'fresh root of Eternity', and ends
by reconciling these two metaphors and articulating a vision
of re-entering eternity through the cycle of nature, as the
speaker envisions her 'mouldering corpse' nourishing new
boughs, 'Where that perished sapling used to be'. Both of
these poems develop a myth of return, a return to nature,
to the harmony from which the self has been exiled, and
to the integrity of death.

Throughout her poetry, through the dramatic personae
of the Gondal poems, or through the lyric 'I' of the non-
Gondal verse, Emily Brontë constantly articulates a sense
of constraint, limitation, and restriction. Her poems also
represent and explore ways of rising above or transcending
these limitations. The heroic exiles and outcasts of Gondal
rise above the limitations of their situations by rebelling
against their society and taking political and military power
into their own hands. In the non-Gondal poems the restrictions on the active life provide an impetus for an intense
focus on the inner life, and in particular for an exploration
of those inner resources of vision and imagination which
might be a means of rising above the external limitations
of the female condition. Death is also constantly invoked
and explored, not as the object of the suicide's desire
(although it sometimes has this aspect), but as a kind
of ideal – akin to the out-of-body experience of vision

– a liberator from restriction, reconciler of contradiction, and restorer of self-integrity.

Emily Brontë's poems are sometimes melodramatic or strident, and sometimes marked by an impressive lyrical intensity. They demonstrate the power that resides in articulation, while at the same time exploring the sources, problems, and possibilities of that power. Despite all their undoubted unevenness they consistently articulate those fears, frustrations and sense of weakness which the poet felt to be peculiarly her own, but which our hindsight might see as being more widely shared by nineteenth-century women.

5 Gender and Genre in *Wuthering Heights*: Gothic Plot and Domestic Fiction

'In spite of much power and cleverness, in spite of its truth to life in the remote corners of England – *Wuthering Heights* is a disagreeable story. The Bells seem to affect painful and exceptional subjects – the misdeeds or oppression of tyranny, the eccentricities of "woman's fantasy".' (*Athenaeum* 25 Dec., 1847, CH, 218)

Most commentators on *Wuthering Heights*, whether critics or devotees, have been struck by the novel's extraordinary power and idiosyncratic nature, its 'eccentricities of "woman's fantasy"'. Many have followed Charlotte Brontë's lead, attributing its strange power to the mysterious vision of an isolated Romantic genius. The novel, wrote Charlotte Brontë in her Preface to the second edition,

was hewn in a wild workshop, with simple tools, out of homely materials. The statuary found a granite block on the moor; gazing thereon, he saw how from the crag might be elicited a head, savage, swart, sinister; a form modelled with at least one element of grandeur – power. He wrought with a rude chisel, and from no model but the vision of his meditations. (WH, 41)

This mythologising of the novel's origins, which seems to have been designed to explain it to a genteel, Southern audience, presents *Wuthering Heights* as the fortuitous conjunction of nature and intense visionary experience in which the shaping process of art plays little part.

There are, however, more mundane sources for this novel than those suggested by Charlotte Brontë. Emily Brontë's bizarre narrative, with its intense passions, inter-familial rivalries, and revenge plot, may have originated in actual family histories of which she knew. Brontë's plot has a number of similarities to the stories which she would have heard, during her brief stay at Law Hill school, about Jack Sharp, its sometime owner, and the Walkers of Walterclough Hall. The rivalry between the usurping adopted son, Jack Sharp, and a natural son; Sharp's systematic degradation of a Walker nephew, and his subsequent decline and bankruptcy are all echoed in the plot of *Wuthering Heights* (See WG, 76ff. and 220ff.).

Others have suggested that the novel owes a great deal to the strange Irish stories with which Patrick Brontë diverted his children at breakfast. In particular, Edward Chitham in *The Brontës' Irish Background* (1986) has argued that the story of the orphan's vengeance is derived from the story of Hugh Brunty, Patrick Brontë's father, who was adopted and subsequently ill-treated by an uncle called Welsh. Welsh himself is a sort of Heathcliff figure: an orphan, discovered on a boat travelling from Liverpool, and adopted by Hugh's grandfather, he later ousted the legitimate heirs from their home and married the daughter of the house.

The tale of 'The Bridegroom of Barna', published in *Blackwood's* in 1840, may also have been a source for Emily Brontë's novel. Certainly it has a very similar plot to *Wuthering Heights*, and concerns the star-crossed love of the children of rival families. Ellen Nugent and

Hugh Lawlor, the heroine and hero of this violent tale are, like Catherine and Heathcliff, united only in death when they are finally buried in a single grave. If Emily Brontë's plot did not spring fully formed from the isolated depths of her imagination, neither did her broader themes and techniques. The fictional transformation of the late eighteenth-century histories which supply some of the elements of the novel's plot, has much in common with other recent and contemporary literature. This is partly a matter of direct influence from Emily Brontë's own reading, but it is also indicative of the ways in which individual artists (no matter how geographically isolated, nor how idiosyncratic) participate in a shared cultural language, and work with shared forms and patterns.

One of my concerns in this chapter will be to suggest that *Wuthering Heights* is not, as F.R. Leavis argues in *The Great Tradition*, 'a kind of sport' – an interesting but minor divergence from the high road of the mainstream English Novel. Instead I want to look at *Wuthering Heights* in the context of the developing traditions of late eighteenth- and early nineteenth-century fiction, and to suggest that the peculiar generic mix of this novel offers a number of interesting perspectives on the whole question of the relationship of the woman writer to the history and tradition of fiction.

Wuthering Heights straddles literary traditions and genres. It combines elements of the Romantic tale of evil-possession, and Romantic developments of the eighteenth-century Gothic novel, with the developing Victorian tradition of Domestic fiction in a realist mode. Its use of the ballad and folk material, romance forms and the fantastic, its emphasis on the passions, its view of childhood, and the representation of the romantic quest for selfhood and of aspiring individualism, all link the novel with Romanticism. On the other hand, the novel's movement towards a renewed emphasis on community and duty, and towards an idealisation of the family seem to be more closely related to the emerging concerns of Victorian fiction. Emily Brontë's novel mixes these various traditions and genres in a number of interesting ways, sometimes fusing and sometimes juxtaposing them. I want to direct attention to the ways in which the novel's mixing of genres may be related to issues of gender by examining some of the ways in which specific historic genres may be related to particular historic definitions of gender.

If Emily Brontë's poems are, as her sister suggested, 'not at all like the poetry women generally write', her novel is at once both very similar to and very different from, the kinds of fiction generally written by women in the early nineteenth century. Indeed, much of the distinctiveness of Emily Brontë's novel may be attributed to the particular ways in which it negotiates different literary traditions, and both combines and explores two major fictional genres – the Gothic and Domestic fiction – which are usually associated with the female writers of the period, although by no means confined to them.

Wuthering Heights has proved impossible to categorise, and continues to confront its readers with a sometimes alarming sense of disorientation, a feeling of finding themselves in 'really different novels'.[1] The novel begins in fictional territory which is reasonably familiar to readers of the eighteenth- and nineteenth-century Domestic novel: a date (1801), the genteel narrator's ironic description of a social visit, the careful description of the domestic interior at the Heights, and the beginnings of an investigation of a code of manners and a particular way of life. However, even in the opening chapter the codes and conventions of polite fiction do not seem adequate either to comprehend or represent life at the Heights. For example, Lockwood's description focuses on the *absence* of the *expected* 'glitter of saucepans and tin cullenders on the walls' (WH, 47), and the presence of 'villainous old guns, and a couple of horse pistols'. Certainly, by the second and third chapters, the genteel narrator and the reader find their generic and social expectations increasingly at odds with the literary genre and social world into which the narrative has moved. The appearance of Catherine's ghost, and Heathcliff's passionate response, take the novel into the literary genre of Gothic and the forms of the fantastic which provide much of its extraordinary power.

The Earnshaw–Heathcliff–Linton plot is a legend-like tale of an old family disrupted by the arrival of Heathcliff, a dark child of mysterious origins who is brought from Liverpool to the Heights by Mr Earnshaw. Nelly Dean's version of this history is almost literally a 'family romance':[2] a story of changing familial and inter-familial relationships; of sibling rivalry between Heathcliff and Hindley; of the intensely close brother–sister relationship of Catherine and Heathcliff, the children of nature and comrades-in-arms against the adult tyranny of Joseph and later of Hindley, the new owner of the Heights.

The theme of active male competition begun in Heathcliff and Hindley is continued beyond the Earnshaw family in Edgar Linton and Heathcliff's rivalry for the attentions of Catherine. Catherine's preference for the more cultivated Edgar precipitates Heathcliff's disappearance, and when he subsequently returns in the guise of a fine and prosperous gentleman he once more disrupts family stability, threatening Catherine and Edgar's fragile marriage, setting in train an elaborate plan of revenge against both the Earnshaw and the Linton families, and eloping with Edgar's sister Isabella. Nelly's account of Heathcliff's destruction of Hindley and his brutalisation of Hindley's son Hareton, the almost parodic violence of his hanging of Isabella's dog, and his callous treatment of his wife and son represents him as a Gothic villain, a demonic, almost otherworldly figure. This fantastic, demonic version of Heathcliff is reinforced by the melodramatic scenes surrounding Catherine's death, and in the final stages of the narrative when he appears to be communing with the spirit of the dead Catherine in preparation for a removal to her sphere.

Embedded within this Gothic framework, however, is a second narrative, which seems to move progressively in the direction of Victorian Domestic Realism. The second half of the novel's double plot – the second generation story of Linton Heathcliff, Hareton Earnshaw and Catherine Linton – appears to move from Gothic beginnings, in which a monstrous Hareton implicitly collaborates in the abduction of Catherine, her forced marriage to Linton and her effective imprisonment at the Heights, to the conventional closure of a dominant form of the Victorian Domestic novel, in which the hero (Hareton) and heroine (Catherine) overcome the obstacles of an obstructive society and withdraw into a private realm of domesticity, where social, co-operative values are renewed within the bosom of the family. In this case the pattern of closure is completed by the planned removal of Hareton and Catherine from the Heights to Thrushcross Grange.

Gothic is usually taken to be the dominant genre of the first generation plot of *Wuthering Heights*, and is associated with its Romanticism, its mystical, fantastic and supernatural elements, and its portrayal of wild nature. In the eighteenth and nineteenth centuries Gothic was a genre particularly identified with women writers, and many recent feminist critics have argued that Female Gothic may be seen as a complex genre which simultaneously represents women's fears and offers fantasies of escape from them.[3] Female Gothic enacts fantasies of female power in the heroine's courage and enterprise, while simultaneously, or by turns, representing the female condition as both confinement and refuge. Many of the Gothic elements of *Wuthering Heights* may be seen as examples of Female Gothic's representation and investigation of women's fears about the private domestic space which is at once refuge and prison. Indeed, Catherine Earnshaw's story might almost be read as an archetypal example of the genre. After a childhood which alternates between domestic confinement and freely roaming the unconfined spaces of the moors, Catherine's puberty is marked by her confinement to the couch of Thrushcross Grange. Womanhood and marriage to Edgar further confine her within the genteel household, and the denouement of her particular Gothic plot involves her imprisonment in increasingly confined spaces: the house, her room, and finally 'this shattered prison' (WH, 196), her body, from which she longs to escape as she does from womanhood itself.

Similarly the story of Isabella Linton focuses on the female lot as a choice between degrees and varieties of imprisonment, as Isabella flees the stifling confinement of the genteel household for a more brutal domestic incarceration at the Heights, now a stronghold of male violence (ch. 17). The first two stages of the history of Catherine Linton follow a similar pattern to Isabella's. Although as a spirited young woman she chafes against the bonds of gentility and the over-protected environment of the Grange, Catherine comes to reassess her former prison as a shelter after her enforced marriage to Linton Heathcliff. The Cathy whom Lockwood observes in the early stages of his narrative is, effectively, a household prisoner, constrained not simply by her own terror and Heathcliff's brute force, but also by contemporary matrimonial laws and her father-in-law's financial power. In changing her role from that of dependent daughter to wife she has ceased to be the legal property of her father and has become instead the property of her husband. When she is both widowed and orphaned she comes under the legal control of her father-in-law, Heathcliff. This legal control of women plays an important part in the novel's plot, and is vividly illustrated in a scene from the marriage of Heathcliff and Isabella.

'If you are called upon in a court of law you'll
remember her language Nelly! And take a good look at
that countenance – she's near the point which would suit
me. No, you're not fit to be your own guardian, Isabella,
now; and I, being your legal protector, must retain you in
my custody, however distasteful the obligation may be.'
(WH, 188–9)

Female Gothic explores women's power and powerlessness, their confinement within the domestic space, their role
in the family, and their regulation by marriage and property
laws not of their own making and, at this point in history,
beyond their power to alter. Many of these concerns are
represented, from a different perspective, in the increasingly
dominant female genre of Domestic fiction. In a fascinating
study of twentieth-century popular Gothics Tania Modleski
has suggested that these similarities make for a continuity
between Gothic and Domestic, since both are 'concerned
with the (often displaced) relationships among family members and with driving home to women the importance of
coping with enforced confinement and the paranoid fears
it generates' (Modleski, 20).

Certainly, in *Wuthering Heights* Gothic and Domestic
are continuous, not simply because of this shared project,
but also because the genres are mixed so as to produce a
structural continuity. For example, although the Gothic is
usually associated with the first generation plot and the
Domestic with the second (or even with the last phase of
the second generation plot), the novel's narrative structure,
and particularly its dislocated chronology, tends to blur
the boundaries between generations and genres. Emily
Brontë's adaptation of the conventions of the Gothic
frame tale is a particularly important element in this
process. In earlier Gothic novels the central narrative is
approached by way of diaries, letters and other documents
which are transcribed or edited by the narrator(s) of the

story. Similarly, the reader approaches the central narrative of *Wuthering Heights* via an outsider, Lockwood, who transmits or mediates Nelly's inner (and insider) narrative. To gain access to the extraordinary stories of the families of Wuthering Heights and Thrushcross Grange the reader must thus pass through, and ultimately pass beyond, the perceptual structures of a bemused genteel male narrator who mediates between the public world he shares with his readers and the inner, private, domestic world conveyed to him by Nelly's stories.

Lockwood's mediation of Nelly's narrative reproduces, as N.M. Jacobs points out, that separation between the male and female spheres which lies at the heart of the novel's action, and also actively involves the reader in the process by which 'domestic reality is obscured by layers of conventional ideology'.[4] This narrative layering also serves to close the gap between inner and outer, private and public, domestic and Gothic. Lockwood's framing narrative is particularly important here, since many of the Gothic horrors displayed to and by Lockwood are in fact supported by the ideology of the culture he represents. His own views of marriage and of women, shown in his romantic fantasies about Cathy, and his cold withdrawal from his flirtation with the young lady at the Spa town, reveal this genteel commentator to be just as manipulative and selfish as the apparently demonic Heathcliff. Lockwood's own genteel ideology in fact sanctions the domestic tyranny whose everyday details he appears to find so foreign and extraordinary as he reports them.

The reader's perceptions of what Lockwood reports is persistently at odds with what the narrator himself sees or expects to see. For example, when he visits the Heights and attempts to engage politely with its owner, Lockwood converses in platitudes derived from the Victorian ideology of the home as refuge from the harsh competitive outside world. The scene he reports is quite at odds with the language in which he congratulates Heathcliff on being 'surrounded by your family and with your amiable lady as the presiding genius over your home and heart' (WH, 55). When he is disabused of this particular conventionalised domestic framework Lockwood's second attempt at comprehending the domestic scene is equally wide of the mark: he assumes that Hareton is the 'favoured possessor of the beneficent fairy'. Heathcliff's bitterly amused riposte, 'We neither of us have the privilege of owning your good fairy', of course goes right to the ideological heart of the matter, since legally Heathcliff does own his daughter-in-law.

Although there is a lack of perceptual fit between Lockwood's language and the domestic reality at the Heights, there is no essential lack of fit between the domestic scene he describes and the ideology of domesticity. Lockwood's expectations emphasise one side of the domestic ideal – the harmonious family presided over by the beneficent fairy who submits to her husband's (father's, brother's or father-in-law's) legal and financial control, in exchange for domestic power as the presiding genius of the tea table. However, the domestic reality of the Heights (as witnessed by Lockwood, or experienced by the two Catherines and Isabella) emphasises the other side of this ideal – the inequalities of the exchange and the implicit tyranny of the structure. One major effect of Brontë's adaptation of the Gothic frame tale in this novel is to locate the domestic as the source of the Gothic.

The structural continuity of Gothic and Domestic is also seen in the way in which the second generation plot supposedly replays the first generation story. *Wuthering Heights* tells the same story twice. Leo Bersani is not alone in feeling that the story is diminished in the retelling, and that the novel declines into a 'rather boring second half . . . the cozy and conventionalized romance between the young Catherine and Hareton Earnshaw'.[5] Others, most notably recent feminist critics, have argued that the novel does not simply repeat the same story, but that it revises it, rewriting the Gothic first generation plot as a Domestic novel.

What is involved in the retelling, and what is the significance of the rewriting? Some feminist critics offer an analysis of the revision which in essence seems to reach the same conclusions as Bersani but via a different route. Rosemary Jackson, for example, sees the revision as a loss of power which signifies inauthenticity and a retreat into compromise as *Wuthering Heights* harnesses Gothic 'to serve and not subvert a dominant ideology' and ultimately silences its fantastic or Gothic elements 'in the name of establishing a normative bourgeois realism'.[6] Similarly, Sandra Gilbert and Susan Gubar argue that by the end of the novel, 'The Heights – hell – has been converted into the Grange – heaven –; and with patriarchal history redefined, renovated, restored, the nineteenth century can truly begin' (Gilbert and Gubar (a), 302). Carol Senf, on the other hand, interprets the revision, more affirmatively, as offering an evolutionary 'version of history that is both more feminine and more egalitarian, a history in which women are no longer the victims of patriarchal authority'.[7] Read in these ways *Wuthering Heights* is either a novel of conformity to dominant ideologies of class and gender, or a novel of protest against, or reformation of, those ideologies.

However, more complex and inclusive possibilities are offered if we read *Wuthering Heights'* movement from Gothic to Domestic Romance in relation to the rise of 'feminine authority' in the novel and the feminisation of nineteenth-century literary culture in general. Nancy Armstrong, in *Desire and Domestic Fiction* (1987), and Jane Spencer in *The Rise of the Woman Novelist* (1986), have both attempted to trace the development of 'a view of writing that links it to the feminine role rather than opposing [it]', and which 'encouraged the expansion of women's professional writing' (Spencer, ix). Both Spencer and Armstrong argue that women novelists gained acceptance and 'authority' only 'at the price of agreeing to keep within the feminine sphere' (Spencer, 107), as defined by their culture. This process of feminisation, which began with the eighteenth-century novel, increasingly defined literature 'as a special category supposedly outside the political arena, with an influence on the world as indirect as women's was supposed to be' (Spencer, xi). In particular the emergence of the novel of courtship and domestic life gave a new value and meaning to the female experience and sensibility. In almost a single move women's experience becomes both absolutely central (to literature) and utterly marginal (to politics).

Clearly this view of literature positioned women writers in a particular way. Any woman who attempted to enter this discourse of literature was faced with a choice of responses: she could accept the dominant definitions of the feminine and write within them; or she could refuse those definitions and attempt either to escape or transcend them, or to engage with and rebel against them. In its mixing and juxtaposing of genres *Wuthering Heights*, perhaps, employs or acknowledges all of these strategies. The revisionary double plotting of this novel does not simply involve a straightforward change of genre from Gothic (the genre of escape or protest) to Domestic (the genre of conformity), but rather its generic and generational shifts are also the structural embodiment of that tendency of Female Gothic – noted by Tania Modleski – which serves to 'convince women that they will not be victims the way their mothers were' (Modleski, 83).

The closing stages of the narrative seem to move towards the conventional closure of the Victorian Domestic novel: the restitution of family fortunes, the restoration of disrupted stability, and intimations of protracted domestic bliss in the protected space of the ideal nuclear family. However, as with so many aspects of this novel, appearances are deceptive. Although the second generation story revises the Gothic plot of the first generation in the direction of

Domestic fiction, the Gothic is not simply written out or obliterated in the process. The Gothic persists in the person of Heathcliff who spans both generations. Indeed, his necrophilia and otherworldliness become more pronounced as the Domestic plot reaches its resolution. The Gothic persists too in the power of Catherine and Heathcliff which remains in the outer narrative, beyond the closure of the Catherine–Hareton plot.

Moreover the 'conventional' Domestic romance with which the novel ends not only revises the initial Gothic plot but is also a revisionary form of the genre in which it purports to be written. In the closing stages of the narrative Catherine Linton, who has previously suffered from the powerlessness imposed on her by a patriarchal legal system, family structures, and dominant views of the feminine, learns to use some of the power that lies in her own abilities. Her book-knowledge (gained from her relatively and unusually free access to her father's library) empowers her against Heathcliff. She can both conduct a witty war of words with him, and can signify her imaginative freedom by taking refuge in a book. In turn she empowers Hareton by helping him to read, and thus both civilises him and imparts practical skills which enable him to reclaim his birthright. Catherine's civilising of Hareton is an interesting variant of a common scene in eighteenth- and nineteenth-century fiction in which a male character offers improving reading to an 'ignorant' (but improvable) female. It is also interesting to note that Catherine's cultivation or 'feminisation' of her cousin coincides with Heathcliff's final decline into an otherworldliness which diverts him from completing his plans to gain total control of the Heights and the Grange. As the novel ends Catherine is about to regain control of her inheritance, and although at this period she would have been legally required to hand all her property back to Hareton when he became her husband, it is nevertheless at least of symbolic importance that Hareton's patrimony is returned to him via the female line. Like Jane Eyre's legacy, the restoration of Catherine's property equalises the balance of power between marriage partners. A degree of financial independence for the female partner seems to be a prerequisite for the companionate marriages with which both these novels end.

In its transition from patriarchal tyranny, masculine competition, domestic imprisonment and the Gothic to the revised Domestic romance of the courtship and companionate marriage of Catherine and Hareton, *Wuthering Heights* both participates in, and engages with, the feminisation of literature and the wider culture noted by Armstrong and Spencer. However, I would suggest that Emily Brontë's novel does not simply reflect or represent this process, but that it also investigates and explores it. The narrative disruptions, the dislocations of chronology, the mixing of genres and Brontë's historical displacement of her story, published in 1847 but set in a carefully dated period leading up to and just beyond 1801, combine to produce a novel which goes back and traces both changing patterns of fiction and the emergence of new forms of the family.

Wuthering Heights traces the emergence of the characteristic form of Victorian fiction – the Domestic novel in realist mode. Its own mixing of genres emphasises the links of this newly dominant form with Gothic and also foregrounds the romance elements of the realistic Domestic novel. The 'cozy conventionalised romance' of Catherine and Hareton is an extremely simplified version of the Domestic romance, which exposes and explores the mechanisms of the form. In other words, the self-conscious idealisation of the Catherine–Hareton story exposes the ideological component of both Emily Brontë's story and of the genre in which it is written.

In its movement between generations and genres *Wuthering Heights* also traces the emergence of the modern family in idealised form. It traces the process, minutely documented by Leonore Davidoff and Catherine Hall in *Family Fortunes* (1987), by which the modern nuclear family (represented by Catherine and Hareton) replaced the larger and more loosely related household (as exemplified by various stages of domestic life at the Heights), withdrawing to a private domestic space removed from the workplace. Catherine and Hareton are shown as inhabiting this newly privatised domestic realm even before their marriage and removal to the Grange. Their cultivation of the flower garden and Hareton's primrose-strewn porridge (WH, 348) are emblematic of their transformation of the Heights into a domain of feminine values, a haven of tranquillity to which men retire from a workaday world of business and competition, in order to cultivate their gardens, their hobbies and the domestic ideal.

However, at the same time as *Wuthering Heights* traces the emergence of the modern family and its hegemonic fictional form of Domestic realism, other elements of the novel – its disrupted chronology, its dislocated narrative structure, and the persistence of the disturbing power of Catherine and Heathcliff – work together to keep other versions of domestic life before the reader: the domestic space as prison, the family as site of primitive passions, violence, struggle and control. In its mixing of genres and in the particular genres it chooses to mix *Wuthering Heights* may, perhaps, be placed with those female fictions which, as Judith Lowder Newton argues 'both support and resist ideologies which have tied middle-class women to the relative powerlessness of their lot and which have prevented them from having a true knowledge of their situation'.[8]

6 Changing the Names: the Two Catherines

> It was a Testament, in lean type, and smelling dreadfully musty: a fly-leaf bore the inscription – "Catherine Earnshaw, her book", and a date some quarter of a century back.
>
> I shut it, and took up another, and another, till I had examined all. Catherine's library was select, and its state of dilapidation proved it to have been well used, though not altogether for a legitimate purpose; scarcely one chapter had escaped a pen and ink commentary – at least, the appearance of one – covering every morsel of blank that the printer had left. Some were detached sentences; other parts took the form of a regular diary. . . . (WH, 62)

These books discovered by Lockwood are the only self-authored records left by Catherine Earnshaw-Linton. Catherine's diary is a text of discontent and rebellion, recording and speaking out against the domestic tyranny of Hindley and the religious tyranny of Joseph. It is also quite literally a marginal text, scrawled in the margins and on the fly-sheets of her well-used library. The childish scribblings arouse in Lockwood an 'immediate interest for the unknown Catherine, and I began, forthwith, to decypher her faded hieroglyphics'. The process of deciphering begun by Lockwood is continued in Nelly's narrative and is repeated by the reader who, like Lockwood, experiences Catherine as a text. Indeed much of *Wuthering Heights* is concerned with deciphering the traces of Catherine Earnshaw. The writing Lockwood finds scratched into the paint on the ledge of his sleeping quarters at the Heights foreshadows an important strand of the narrative structure.

> This writing was nothing but a name repeated in all kinds of characters, large and small – *Catherine Earnshaw*, here and there varied to *Catherine Heathcliff*, and then again to *Catherine Linton*. (WH, 61)

The names Lockwood deciphers circulate through the text, and one of the reader's tasks is to decipher them afresh, to explore the significance of both the names and the roles which attach to them. The first Catherine begins life as Catherine Earnshaw and ends it as Catherine Linton. Catherine Heathcliff remains an unfulfilled possibility, a route not taken, although some would argue that this unoccupied term in fact names Catherine's true identity, and that she acquires this name-role beyond the narrative when her spirit joins with Heathcliff's to wander the moors eternally. Catherine's daughter, on the other hand, occupies each of the names in turn and traces back the route to her mother's first name. The novel thus begins and ends with Catherine Earnshaw. However, although the names circulate through the text they create a pattern of asymmetrical repetition rather than of circularity. The stories of the two Catherines, the similarities and differences in their shapes, form a central strand in the elaborately patterned system of repetitions and differences which make this novel's structure.

The story of the first Catherine hinges – as do most novels of the period – on her choice between two men. Choosing the correct husband is the central moral task set for the heroine of most eighteenth- and nineteenth-century novels, particularly those written by women. Catherine's choice of Edgar is socially sanctioned and conforms to the dominant fictional pattern (seen most clearly and familiarly in the novels of Jane Austen) according to which heroines are led to make the rational choice of the sensible, educated man of property and standing in the community. Catherine's self-professed reasons for marrying Edgar are couched in the terms of rationality and prudence:

> "Because he is handsome and pleasant to be with . . . because he loves me . . . And he will be rich, and I shall like to be the greatest woman of the neighbourhood, and I shall be proud of having such a husband." (WH, 118)

However, *Wuthering Heights* departs from fictional and social norms by exploring the consequences of the socially sanctioned choice. In Catherine's case, marriage is not the answer to the problem of her life, the resolver of all contradictions, as it usually is in Domestic and romantic fiction. On the contrary, marriage compounds the problems of Catherine's life, and exposes its contradictions. The return of Heathcliff in the later stages of Catherine's story exposes the inadequacies of an apparently appropriate marriage, and raises questions about both the nature of the choice Catherine had been required to make, and the capacity of genteel marriage to comprehend all of a woman's needs. Emily Brontë's particular treatment of the Catherine–Edgar–Heathcliff plot seems to question the fictional paradigm which structures a woman's life as a choice between two men.

Catherine's fundamental inability to choose between Edgar and Heathcliff not only raises the question 'what does a woman want?', but more profoundly engages with the 'riddle of femininity', 'what we men call "the enigma of woman" '.[1] The novel explores the question 'what is a woman?' by charting the process by which Catherine learns to be a woman as defined by the society in which she lives, and by tracing the difficulties which she experiences in living as a woman thus defined. As a motherless, and subsequently fatherless, girl growing up in a geographically isolated and loosely organised working household, Catherine reaches puberty relatively untrammelled by parental notions of suitable feminine conduct. Her childhood is, on the whole, spent with Heathcliff in a private, unsocialised and ungendered moorland world. Her encounters with adult authority, in the form of her brother's petty domestic tyranny and Joseph's rigid Methodism, develop her capacity for rebellion and resistance, and she thus becomes an assertive child associated with the realm of nature, its freedom and power, rather than with the domestic and its constraints.

Emily Brontë's portrayal of Catherine's sudden and dramatic transformation into a genteel young lady during her stay at Thrushcross Grange focuses on the way in which the particular version of femininity involved in the ideal of female gentility is socially produced and reinforced, rather than derived from women's 'nature'. Catherine's transformation, described by Nelly as a 'reform' (WH, 93) is shown as, in fact, a process of formation or construction. Frances Earnshaw, acting under Mrs Linton's guidance and 'employing art not force', performs the 'maternal' function of subjecting her sister-in-law to a 'due restraint' and shaping an acceptably feminine Catherine:

> trying to raise her self-respect with fine clothes and flattery, which she took readily, so that instead of a wild, hatless little savage jumping into the house, and rushing to squeeze us all breathless, there alighted from a handsome black pony a very dignified person with brown ringlets falling from the cover of a feathered beaver. (WH, 93)

Nelly's observations on the social climbing of the newly transformed Catherine provide an unwitting comment on the self-division, the 'perplexities and untold troubles' (WH, 108), that attend the role of the 'proper lady'.

Catherine's ambition, we are told, 'led her to adopt a *double character* without exactly intending to deceive anyone' (WH, 107, my emphasis). Catherine's ambivalence about her new role and her continued identification with Heathcliff suggest how profoundly at odds it is with her own nature. Catherine's famous assertion that Heathcliff is 'more myself than I am. Whatever our souls are made of, his and mine are the same' (WH, 121) is perhaps as much a statement of her identification with an earlier, pre-gendered version of herself, as it is a declaration of elemental passion. The adult Catherine persistently yearns for the self-consistency of the girlhood state that pre-existed the self-divisions induced by her education into the class-gender role of the genteel lady.

> 'I wish I were a girl again, half savage, and hardy and free; and laughing at injuries, not maddening under them! Why am I so changed? . . . I'm sure I should be myself were I once among the heather on those hills! (WH, 163)

Whether in her role as a child of nature, or in her uneasy guise of 'proper lady', Catherine Earnshaw is presented as a powerful woman. Even the unsympathetic Nelly concedes that at 'fifteen she was the queen of the countryside; she had no peer' (WH, 106). The 'haughty, headstrong creature' is a kind of Yorkshire Gondal's Queen whose attitude to Edgar and Heathcliff is reminiscent of A.G.A.'s scornful wielding of female power over her lovers. Catherine's power, and the role it plays in shaping her story, may usefully be seen in the context of the issue of female power (what it is and how to use it) which was being debated in the conduct books, designed to inculcate ideas of appropriately feminine behaviour, and in periodical articles in the early nineteenth century. Women, as Sarah Ellis argued, must relinquish power and the direct control of their own lives.

All that has been expected to be enjoyed from the indulgence of selfishness, must then of necessity be left out of our calculations, with all that ministers to the pride of superiority, all that gratifies the love of power, all that converts the woman into the heroine. (*Advice to The Wives of England*)

The love of power, or 'heroinism', must be yielded in order that women might be able to exercise feminine influence in the domestic sphere.

Women in their position in life must consent to be inferior to men, but as their inferiority consists chiefly in their want of power, this deficiency is abundantly made up to them by their capability of exercising influence. (*Advice to the Daughters of England*)[2]

Catherine's history demonstrates the difficulties of trying to be the heroine of one's own life in a social and domestic milieu which cannot provide a theatre for heroism. If Catherine is an image of female power it is a power which is doomed to find no channel in the social world of the novel, and can only turn on itself. It is interesting that Catherine's power over Heathcliff (and arguably over Edgar too) is greater after her death than it was in life, since her power is essentially transcendent rather than material. Catherine's story not only shows the limits of female power but also explores its problematic nature. The novel repeatedly focuses on the realities of gender politics by focusing on the way that Catherine's sense of personal and emotional power is not a means to authority and the resolving of conflict, but is the cause of conflict with others, and uncertainty and ultimately paranoia in herself. Catherine is granted a licensed power which allows her to exercise a whimsical tyranny. As far as her brother is concerned, as long as she advances the family by a favourable marriage, 'she might trample on [the servants] like slaves' (WH, 128). In addition to exploring the ambivalence of this tyrannical form of female power, the novel also exposes its tendency to become turned against itself, as seen, for example, in Catherine's declaration that 'if I cannot keep Heathcliff for my friend, if Edgar will be mean and jealous, I'll try to break their hearts by breaking my own' (WH, 155).

Catherine's story also dramatises the limits of female influence. Her marriage to Edgar, which ironically she sees as a means of empowering herself to assist Heathcliff (WH, 122), proves unable to reconcile the two men, and her belief in the power of her influence over Heathcliff is equally illusory. In short, Catherine's story vividly illustrates the fact that no matter how powerful and ruling her personality, a woman, as defined in nineteenth-century ideologies of gender and the family, must always cede definition and control to others and she is always, at least potentially, a victim. The spirited and rebellious Catherine must ultimately submit to the legal control of her father, her brother and subsequently her husband. As she passes from childhood she becomes the victim of the ideal of feminine gentility. She also becomes the object of a competitive struggle between two men, each of whom wants her to conform to his own version of her.

Caught uneasily between these conflicting subject positions Catherine is ultimately broken by the pressure of the contradictions. She herself blames Edgar and Heathcliff for her predicament.

'You and Edgar have broken my heart Heathcliff! And you both come to bewail the deed to me as if *you* were the people to be pitied! I shall not pity you, not I. You have killed me – and thriven on it, I think. How strong you are! How many years do you mean to live after I am gone?' (WH, 195)

Catherine's final illness is, in effect, a withdrawal from both the world and the self. Her derangement (WH, 158ff.) enacts her experience of self-alienation. She is unable to recognise the reflection in the mirror as her own, and she regresses to a childhood state, to the Edenic unproblematic period of undivided and undifferentiated selfhood before she became a battleground for conflicting versions of womanhood.

Like so many women in Victorian fiction Catherine dies in childbirth and is thus not required to negotiate that other profoundly ideological version of womanhood – 'the mother'. However, although she has been long dead when the novel's action begins Catherine Earnshaw-Linton persists in the dramatic present of the novel, in the spirit form that haunts Heathcliff and which initiates Lockwood into some of the profundities and mysteries of life at the Heights. Her presence also persists, significantly modified, in the person of her daughter,

> the most winning thing that ever brought sunshine into a desolate house – a real beauty in face – with the Earnshaws' handsome dark eyes, but the Lintons' fair skin, and small features . . . Her spirit was high, though not rough, and qualified by a heart sensitive and lively to excess in its affections. That capacity for intense attachments reminded me of her mother; still she did not resemble her, for she could be soft and mild as a dove, and she had a gentle voice, and pensive expression: her anger was never fierce; it was deep and tender. (WH, 224)

If Cathy is a repetition of her mother, she is also a variation. Whereas the older Catherine's childhood prepares her for the role of Gondal's Queen, 'half savage, and hardy, and free', her daughter is the spoiled, wilful, and pert fairy tale princess, the empress of her walled domain and mistress of her father and his servants. As the only daughter of a

bookish widower she receives a wider education than was
perhaps common for girls of the period, but in other respects
her life is extremely constricted and protected, and contrasts
markedly with her mother's childhood.

> Till she reached the age of thirteen, she had not
> once been beyond the range of the park by herself . . .
> Gimmerton was an unsubstantial name in her ears; the
> chapel, the only building she had approached or entered,
> except her own home. (WH, 224-5)

In some senses Cathy's story reverses rather than repeats
her mother's. For example, whereas the first Catherine's
puberty is marked by a rite of passage from the Heights to
the Grange, and from rebellious childhood to constrainedly
genteel adolescence, her daughter makes the journey in
reverse. Cathy's first acquaintance with the Heights, like her
mother's with the Grange, is the result of an act of curiosity
and rebellion which has misfired. Cathy finds herself at the
Heights after illicitly attempting to reach the enchanted and
forbidden territory of Penistone Crags, whose 'golden rocks'
have hitherto marked the physical limits of her horizon and
the boundary of her childhood obedience.

While economic dependency, a precarious family position, and the confusions arising from her precipitate
education into the role of genteel young lady all combine
to propel Catherine into marriage with Edgar; economic
security, restricted and over-protected family circumstances, and the steady imbibing of the principles of
self-sacrificing feminine gentility render Cathy extremely
susceptible to Heathcliff's duplicity, and his son's whining
vulnerability. Where Catherine apparently made her choice
of Edgar freely, Cathy is effectively abducted by Heathcliff
and emotionally blackmailed into submission by her
cousin Linton, who interestingly employs the supposedly
'feminine' strategies previously used by his mother. The

marriage between Cathy and Linton thus makes explicit those aspects of genteel marriage which are implicit in the marriage of Catherine and Edgar, and which contribute to Catherine's demise. However, when Cathy is faced with the full horror of domestic imprisonment and the daily experience of Heathcliff's malevolence, the rebellious streak inherited from her mother helps her to resist mental enslavement. In her imprisonment at the Heights Cathy divests herself of the outward signs and mental attitudes of feminine gentility, and salvages an element of imaginative freedom by refusing to conform to certain of the available definitions of the feminine role – housewife, obedient daughter (daughter-in-law), or genteel ornament – opting instead for the role of unsociable slattern with her nose in a book.

Cathy's rebellion, a proud resistance which acknowledges its limitations while asserting its powers, is revealed in an account of an exchange between Heathcliff and Cathy early in Lockwood's narrative.

> 'And you, you worthless —' . . . 'there you are at your idle tricks again! The rest of them do earn their bread – you live on my charity! Put your trash away, and find something to do.'
>
> 'I'll put my trash away, because you can make me if I refuse,' answered the young lady, closing her book, and throwing it on a chair. 'But I'll not do anything, though you should swear your tongue out, except what I please!' (WH, 72)

Cathy also empowers herself to resist her circumstances by adopting the guise of witch, a term historically used to describe and contain transgressive female power.

> 'I warn you [Joseph] to refrain from provoking me, or I'll ask your abduction as a special favour . . . ,'

she continued, taking a long, dark book from a shelf.
'I'll show you how far I've progressed in the Black Art.'
(WH, 57)

Like her mother's story, Cathy's is structured around
a choice between two men, but Cathy makes her choice
sequentially, and the second choice is informed by her
experience of the consequences of the first. In a sense
Cathy's story replays those of both Isabella and Catherine.
Like Isabella she is lured, by Heathcliff's scheming, from
the petted and suffocating security of the Grange, and
like Isabella she experiences directly the force of his
brutality. More interestingly, the Cathy–Hareton plot
may be seen as a repetition of the Catherine–Heathcliff
plot, in which the younger Catherine acts out her mother's unfulfilled relationship with Heathcliff. Indeed, in
Lockwood's fantasy (WH, 335), Cathy is faced with a
similar choice to her mother's: a choice between the
genteel man of property, currently inhabiting Thrushcross
Grange (Lockwood himself) and the boorish rustic at the
Heights (Hareton). However, this is never more than a
notional choice for the Cathy produced by the particular
history which Emily Brontë has structured for her.
Cathy's experience of the discontents of over-civilisation
in her oppressively restricted genteel life at the Grange
and in Linton's peevish and petted gentility, and her
experience of domestic incarceration at the Heights all
lead to a reassessment of class and gender stereotypes
from which her courtship of Hareton proceeds. Indeed,
it is perhaps Cathy, rather than Catherine, who gives
Emily Brontë the opportunity of writing 'the scene of
choice', in which the heroine chooses and demands her
love, 'giving herself freely and, throwing Jane Austen's
prudence to the winds, declaring her passion' (Moers,
167), which Ellen Moers sees as characteristic of 'every
woman writer who was a feminist in [her depiction of]

love' (Moers, 157). Emily Brontë's juxtapositioning of the stories of the two Catherines calls into question the view of romantic love implied in Moers' formulation, and also probes the uses as well as the limitations of prudence. Cathy's history (like her mother's) illustrates the problems involved in 'throwing . . . prudence to the winds', and is used to explore the dangers involved in women thinking of themselves, or their love, as gifts to be liberally bestowed. In her second marriage Cathy does not *demand* her love, but she chooses freely, after studying Hareton closely, and it is she who initiates their intimacy and nurtures its development.

In the closing stages of the narrative Cathy moves towards occupying spaces and roles previously vacated or refused by her mother. She is to become Catherine Earnshaw, and in doing so will redeem Heathcliff's protégé and other self, Hareton. In the process Cathy relinquishes her role as the victim of a Gothic plot for that of the heroine of a Domestic romance. In this latter role Cathy comes to represent both female power and feminine influence. Although she is trapped and imprisoned by Heathcliff and a patriarchal legal system, Cathy exercises one of the few forms of power available to the powerless – resistance. This initial strategy of resistance frees her to choose a version of the role of feminine influence advocated by the conduct books. In conduct book fashion Catherine reclaims the noble savage Hareton, offering him culture which is – as Terry Eagleton rather nervously puts it – 'unemasculating'.[3]

However, Emily Brontë's presentation of the relationship between Cathy and Hareton offers variations on the pattern of the nurturing female. Unlike the conduct book females, Cathy is not all sweet virtue. Although she is (as is so often the case in the Victorian novel) the stimulus for Hareton's cultural ambition, she also mocks and frustrates his efforts to teach himself to read, causing him to burn the small library he has acquired (WH, 333). When Cathy regrets her former actions she adopts 'feminine' strategies of stealth and indirection to rekindle Hareton's interest in books. *Wuthering Heights* is perhaps franker than are the conduct books about the manipulations and particularly the sexual exploitation involved in the exercise of feminine influence. Cathy's cultivation of Hareton is portrayed fairly openly as a form of sexual control. Her gift of the book illustrates the point. Having wrapped a handsome book, she sends it to Hareton via Nelly who is instructed to ' "tell him, if he'll take it I'll come and teach him to read it right . . . and if he refuse it, I'll go upstairs and never trouble him again." ' (WH, 345).

In another interesting variation on the pattern of the conduct book female, and the Domestic romance heroine, Cathy is not made to pay the usual price for her feminine influence, which, according to Judith Lowder Newton, 'was made contingent upon the renunciation of such self-advancing forms of power as control or self-definition' (Lowder Newton, 4). In exercising influence over Hareton, Cathy is also resuming control of her own life and defining herself anew. Her early history has demonstrated (to the character and the reader) the limitations of feminine gentility, and her later history shows how just as this cultural construct is learned it can be unlearned. Having learned to divest herself of many of the forms of feminine gentility, Cathy reconstructs both herself and Hareton. Whereas Catherine is destroyed by her inability to reconcile conflicting images of herself, and the contradictory definitions of the feminine which confront her, Cathy negotiates them and ultimately constructs a new role for herself.

7 Nelly Dean: Memoirs of a Survivor

[T]he housekeeper, a matronly lady taken on as a fixture along with the house. (Lockwood of Nelly, WH, 51)

'I certainly esteem myself a steady, reasonable kind of body . . . I have undergone sharp discipline which has taught me wisdom; and then, I have read more than you would fancy . . . you could not open a book in this library that I have not looked into, and got something out of, unless it be that range of Greek and Latin, and that of French – and those I know from one another: it is as much as you can expect from a poor man's daughter.' (Nelly of herself, WH, 103)

The narrative of *Wuthering Heights* is framed or enclosed by Lockwood's voice, the voice of the novel's dramatic present, but Nelly's is its most persistent voice, the voice of the enclosed, inner, and retrospective narrative. Many recent critics[1] have noted that this narratorial division of labour replicates that of the culture in which the novel was produced. Like nineteenth-century society, the narrative voices of *Wuthering Heights* are divided into 'separate spheres'. The outer, enclosing narrative voice is that of an educated and worldly man of means who occupies a public, social sphere and who assumes a community of shared values with his readers. The voice of the inner, enclosed narrative, on the other hand, is that of a self-educated and socially subordinate woman whose positions as nurse, trusted housekeeper, surrogate sister or mother, give her a privileged access to the intimate lives of virtually all the family units of the novel. In short, Nelly is the narrator of the private domestic life.

Nelly's narrative is presented as a specifically feminine discourse which proceeds, under Lockwood's encouragement, in 'true gossip's fashion' (WH, 103). Whereas Lockwood's narrative perspective is that of the detached, ironic, almost anthropological observer, Nelly's is based on the minute details of lived as well as observed experience. If Nelly is presented as a stereotypical woman, as many have argued, then her tale is, in some ways, a stereotypical 'feminine' narrative with its minute concern for the particularities of everyday domestic life, its circumstantiality and its fond recall of apparently redundant detail.

Nelly is, in part, the wise and canny rustic of the ballad tradition and, like many ballads, her story begins in a haze of meditative reflections on the passage of time, and on the extent of the 'alterations' and 'troubles' she has witnessed. The legendary and potentially melodramatic tale of violence, jealousy, and intrigue which she unravels for Lockwood is, however, embedded in a matrix of Yorkshire common sense. Like Jane Austen's witty and urbane narrator Nelly too has her universally acknowledged truths but, in the absence of the Austenian ironies, Nelly's maxims and adages carry the authority of a specifically feminine wisdom. However, although sound and authentic, Nelly's moral maxims are also – it is widely acknowledged – crucially limited. I shall return shortly to the novel's exploration of the nature and extent of these limitations. For the moment let us consider the apparent paradox that this commonsensical, moralising, and conventionally judgemental narrator should also be widely regarded as the central device in the novel's strategy of making 'conventional moral judgements impossible' (Q.D. Leavis, 119). The whole point of the conventionality of

Nelly's moral judgements, or so it is often argued, is to reveal the inadequacy of such judgements in the face of the elemental forces exposed in the narrative of *Wuthering Heights*.

Nelly's conventionality and her unobtrusiveness are also indispensable to her other narrative tasks. In fact Nelly is the only possible narrator, since she has access to information possessed by no other character, but also, more importantly, as Robert Kiely has pointed out, 'neither Heathcliff nor Lockwood could possibly tell the story without focusing almost exclusively on himself' (Kiely, 236). Nelly's self-effacing and other-directed narrative, on the contrary, is partly a function of gender, and partly of her class position as a servant. Nelly's narrative stance is, for the most part, that of the passive spectator who witnesses the active lives of others. In the narrative economy of *Wuthering Heights*, it seems, men make events while women are the subjects or the tellers of stories.

On the other hand, we might see Nelly's apparent unobtrusiveness not as a female role, but a feminine disguise in which apparent passivity masks a covert activity which is a narrative version of feminine influence working by stealth. James Kavanagh, whose analysis of the novel turns on a particular reading of Nelly which makes her its central figure, argues that Nelly exercises an 'active, even directive control'[2] both as the teller and shaper of the narrative, and as a listener within it. Kavanagh views Nelly's narrative control as both 'opportunistic and self-effacing' (34) and argues that her unobtrusive ' "common sense" ' discourse 'effectively solicits an unnoticed "natural" sympathy' which is exercised on behalf of specific values and interests.

While Kavanagh does not go to the lengths of Q.D. Leavis's despised American professor for whom 'Nelly Dean is Evil' (Q.D. Leavis, 86), he does, nevertheless, like some other recent commentators, make Nelly into the villain of the piece. In general, interpretations of

Nelly's influence on events, her strategies of storytelling and of the nature and significance of her conventional moral pieties, seem to turn on questions of what kind of woman Nelly Dean is and, in particular, on the nature of the conceptions of motherhood and the mother figure which she embodies. On the one hand, Q.D. Leavis offers a condescendingly essentialist view of Nelly as the 'normal maternal woman' (95), whose 'truly feminine nature satisfies itself in nurturing all the children in the book in turn' (93). For others, like Gilbert and Gubar, and Kavanagh, Nelly is not an Earth Mother but the 'Phallic Mother' whose conventional moral pieties represent her internalisation of patriarchy's values. In this version Nelly does not perform a naturally nurturing function, but rather polices the realm of patriarchal culture, deputising for the absent mothers of this novel by taking up the mother's traditional role of preserving and inculcating afresh in each generation the values of patriarchy and the Law of the Father.

It is undoubtedly true that Nelly's history, as we recover it from her narrative, is the story of her progressive co-optation to patriarchal, or more precisely to gentry values, as her early contempt for the milksops Edgar and Isabella and the showy splendours of Thrushcross Grange gives way to an identification with its bookish, ordered culture and 'civilised' values. However, the novel also repeatedly focuses attention on the material realities of Nelly's class position which keep her at a distance from her master and mistress. Unlike most of the novel's protagonists Nelly must and does *work*, and her involvement in the world of work is a central component of her common-sense values. Indeed, the much-discussed emotional and imaginative limitations of Nelly's conventional view of the world might be seen as a means of placing the emotional intensities of the central characters as the self-indulgent and self-referential emotionalism of a leisured class. Nelly's activity about her work detaches her from

the passive intensities and emotional manipulations of her
employers.

> While Miss Linton moped about the park and garden,
> always silent, and almost always in tears; her brother shut
> himself up among books that he never opened . . . with
> a continual vague expectation that Catherine, repenting
> her conduct, would come of her own accord to ask
> pardon . . . – and while *she* fasted pertinaciously, under
> the idea, probably, that . . . pride alone held him from
> running to cast himself at her feet, *I went about my
> household duties*, convinced that the Grange had but one
> sensible soul in its walls, and that lodged in my body.
> (WH, 158, my emphasis)

In fact, Nelly is by turns critic and defender of both the
Linton and the Earnshaw families. This is partly a matter
of the servant's loyalty to 'our family', but it also involves
her loyalty to an idea of the family. The story that Nelly tells
is a family romance. That is to say it is structured around
changing family relationships and the patterns of exchange,
circulation and repetition within and between different
families and different generations of the same family. As
well as narrating this family romance, Nelly also occupies a
key position in the novel's familial structure. Nelly's natural
family is significantly absent from her narrative, and in its
place she has a series of fostering or fostered families.
First, Nelly is foster-sister to Catherine and Hindley,
and shares their sibling rivalry when Heathcliff arrives to
disrupt familial harmony. After old Earnshaw's death her
role changes to that of foster-mother, and is accompanied
by an alteration in her perceptions of individual members
of the family and their relationships.

> [W]hen the children fell ill of the measles and I had to
> tend them, and take on me the cares of a woman at once,

I changed my ideas. Heathcliff was dangerously sick, and
while he lay at the worst he would have me constantly at
his pillow . . .
    He got through, and the doctor affirmed it was
in a great measure owing to me . . . *I was vain of his
commendations*, and softened towards the being by whose
means I earned them, and thus Hindley lost his last ally.
(WH, 79, my emphasis. Note that Nelly's pride in her
new maternal role is directly linked to a desire to please
a male authority figure – the doctor.)

Like the two Catherines (and perhaps also Frances
Earnshaw and Isabella) Nelly enters the state of womanhood
(in her case this is defined as motherhood) prematurely
and precipitately. Nelly continues her mothering role
into the second generation, first assuming charge of
Hareton Earnshaw, the son of her brother/son Hindley,
and subsequently acting as mother to the daughter of
her sister/daughter. Thus, although she is biologically
and legally related to no one in the text Nelly is a
'relative creature', defined and determined by her position
within a system of family relationships as daughter, sister,
wife or mother. Instead of occupying one or other of these
relative positions successively, Nelly occupies several of
them simultaneously, replicating the situation of many
actual Victorian families, including Emily Brontë's own,
in which sisters and daughters were required to deputise
for dead mothers.
    Failure to take account of the complexities of Nelly's
position as a relative creature may lead to an over-simplified
view of her character, and her role in the novel's complex
view of the politics of the family. This complexity is
particularly evident in the contradictions and confusions
of Nelly's attempts to defend the interests of the family
(variously defined), or to advance the interests of individual
members of her numerous and extended surrogate family,

for example, in the already-noted confusion of her loyalties to Hindley and Heathcliff. A similar conflict of loyalties, and confusion about her own position, is evident in the scene (WH, 121) in which Nelly, who becomes aware that Heathcliff is also a hidden listener, is made to listen to Catherine's declaration of the nature of her feelings for Heathcliff and Edgar. Nelly is further embroiled in family politics when her dilemma about leaving Hareton in the increasingly barbaric regime at the Heights is resolved for her by a combination of the patriarchal power of Hindley and Edgar, and the feminine tyranny of Catherine.

> Much against my inclination, I was persuaded to leave Wuthering Heights . . . Little Hareton was nearly five years old, and I had just begun to teach him his letters. We made a sad parting, but Catherine's tears were more powerful than ours. When I refused to go, and when she found that her entreaties did not move me, she went lamenting to her husband and brother. The former offered me munificent wages; the latter ordered me to pack up. He wanted no women in the house . . . And so I had but one choice left, to do as I was ordered . . . I kissed Hareton good-bye; and, since then he has been a stranger, and it's queer to think it, but I've no doubt he has completely forgotten about Ellen Dean and that he was ever more than all the world to her, and she to him. (WH, 128)

I have quoted this passage at length because as well as focusing on the economic, class, and family politics of Nelly's position, it also provides an unobtrusive comment on a little noted aspect of the emotional constraints of her situation. Much of Nelly's down-to-earthness and emotional control, alternatively lauded or despised by modern commentators, may perhaps be seen as the not unsurprising consequence of repeated ruptures in her bonding with her surrogate siblings, ruptures which result from the precariousness of Nelly's position as a female servant.

It is often argued that, despite her avowed reluctance to leave the Heights, Nelly is nevertheless soon converted to a total advocacy of Linton family interests. Certainly she seeks to defend the Linton household from the threats posed by Heathcliff on his return from self-imposed exile. Here, once more, the complex tensions of her multiple familial roles and of her dependent class position subject her to a conflict of loyalties which results, at least according to James Kavanagh, in a betrayal of 'her ostensible protective maternal function in the family romance' as she seems 'willing to sacrifice Cathy as well as Heathcliff, to preserve the sterile Linton regime of family law and order, and her own position within it' (Kavanagh, 62). Nelly is, however, perhaps, less the preserver of Linton family law and order, than the preserver and advocate of an idea of the family. This is shown particularly clearly at the time of Hindley's death when 'ancient associations lingered round [her] heart' and she 'wept as for a blood relation' (WH, 220). On this occasion her loyalty to the Linton regime is subordinated to more general values, as Nelly urges upon Edgar her sense of his and her own obligations.

> I said my old master and foster brother had a claim on my services as strong as his own. Besides, I reminded him that the child, Hareton, was his own wife's nephew, and, in the absence of nearer kin, he ought to act as its guardian; and he ought to and must inquire how the property was left, and look over the concerns of his brother-in-law. (WH, 221)

In this last example, as elsewhere, Nelly seeks to combat the threat posed to the family by Heathcliff's conscious attempts to destroy her own (surrogate) families, and also by his unconscious threat to the idea of family stability as a mysterious outsider whose disruptive energies cannot be contained within its limits. Nelly's narrative is, in part, the story of her active competition with Heathcliff over the definition and survival of the family. In this battle it is Nelly who is the survivor, an image of female resilience, resourcefulness and power. Lockwood's 'human fixture' not only withstands the vicissitudes of the disruptive passions of both generations and both families in the novel, she also mediates between them and, in the tradition of the Shakespearean nurse, presides over the younger generation's resistance to the dead forms of the past, and their renewal of life and love.

Nelly also mediates between two of the novel's formal modes – those of realism and romance. Nelly's down-to-earth language, and the common-sense perspective of the hard-working woman, create a realistic framework for the Gothic events of the earlier part of her narrative, and for the romance elements of the concluding domestic idyll. Nelly also mediates between various class positions; she is the 'poor man's daughter' who works hard for her living and has no home apart from that offered by her current 'family'. While Heathcliff attempts to escape the limitations of his dependent social position by acquiring the income and appearance of a 'gentleman', Nelly invests in the cultural capital of her employer's ample library to add to the stock of her native wisdom and to the sharp lessons administered by the realities of her dependent position. The adventurer's road to self-advancement, which Heathcliff apparently takes, was not open to the female character in Victorian fiction – unless she was a transgressive woman like Thackeray's Becky Sharpe. Nelly's story, more stereotypically female, is one of modest self-help, and *Wuthering Heights* is sufficiently complex in its handling of Nelly's narrative to reveal the emotional costs of a self-improvement pursued in the gaps of the lives of her social superiors and employers.

Nelly's narrative is the memoir of a survivor who, as Carol Senf remarks, recognises and 'generally sides with . . . power or, at least, rarely challenges it openly'.[3] However, if the survivor attempts to coerce the story 'into a more docile and therefore more congenial mode' (Gilbert and Gubar (a), 290), censoring out its more threatening and subversive elements, the tale she has to tell at times resists her efforts to shape it to the survivor's perspective. Nelly's narrative strategies can withstand, constrain, and restrict, but they cannot finally contain the disruptive energies of Catherine and Heathcliff. The more docile story of Cathy and Hareton also resists the narrative shape which Nelly seeks to impose upon it. The mythic version of her Edenic children blossoming under her maternal gaze with which Nelly regales Lockwood on his return to the north (WH, 350ff.) is counteracted by the dramatised scenes from their courtship.

Thus, although Nelly's is the dominant and most persistent voice in the text it is not *the* voice of the text which, with its complex structural interaction of narrative perspectives, speaks with more than one voice. Perhaps we might even see Nelly's narrative itself as polyphonic, speaking with more than one voice, for this female narrative, despite its utterer's self-confessed lack of sympathy with a number of her subjects, nevertheless has a sympathy of attention, and an inclusiveness of detail and perspective, which subverts the narrator's own design.

8 The Male Part of the Poem[1]

Emily Brontë's most recent biographer, Edward Chitham, suggests that 'she did not generally get on well with men', and speculates that she perhaps liked her 'created men' better, even though 'Lockwood, Edgar, Joseph and Hindley all have major faults for the reader to disapprove' (Chitham, 127). Given that Emily Brontë's closest male acquaintance was confined – as far as we are able to tell – to her eccentric and irascible father, an arrogant and dissolute brother, an imperious, acerbic Belgian schoolmaster, and a universally complaisant curate (William Weightman), her failure to 'get on well with men' is perhaps hardly surprising. However, while the author's general views on men no doubt affected the ways in which she wrote about them in her fiction, those views are now irrecoverable, and the processes by which they are mediated in fiction are complex. This chapter will concern itself with the textual representation of men and the masculine domain, and with their role and function in the narrative structure of *Wuthering Heights*.

As I suggested in the previous chapter, the novel's double narrative replicates the separate masculine and feminine spheres of Victorian ideology; the inner, feminine narrative of Nelly Dean has to be approached through, and is mediated by, the outer, masculine narrative of Lockwood. Lockwood is, on the one hand, the reader's representative in the text, as the ordinary person who encounters the extraordinary world which becomes the subject of the story, but he is also the story's censor, who seeks to mould and shape it to his genteel, masculine point of view.

Clearly the novel treats ironically Lockwood's attempts to assimilate everything to his normative perspective. This irony is present right from the beginning when Lockwood mistakes Heathcliff for a kindred spirit – 'I know by instinct his reserve springs from an aversion to showy displays of feeling' (WH, 47). Despite the irony, however, Lockwood's control of the narrative casts him in the role of male authority figure which is reproduced in various forms throughout the novel.

All of the male characters in this novel are clearly associated with authority and/or oppression. Old Mr Earnshaw, Hindley and Edgar are all figures of patriarchal authority. Hindley, like Heathcliff, is also, at particular points, a victim of patriarchal authority, but each is able to change his position in the binary system of oppressor/oppressed which characterises the novel's masculine domain. Hindley, in due course, takes on his father/oppressor's role in the structure of the patriarchal family, and Heathcliff achieves a position of dominance through economic advancement. Even the socially subordinate Joseph, the servant who endlessly quotes Scripture at Nelly and her young charges (in both generations), functions as a representative of repressive patriarchal authority.

Paradoxically, the male is also represented as a disruptive stranger who threatens the stability of the family, that cornerstone of patriarchal society. First, Heathcliff is thrust upon the Earnshaw family by the father, who insists 'You must e'en take it as a gift of God, though it's as dark almost as if it came from the devil' (WH, 77). Largely as a consequence of Heathcliff's initial disruption of the familial order, and his displacement of Hindley in his father's increasingly capricious affection, Hindley becomes estranged from his family and leaves to return as a stranger with a young wife who is also unknown to the family. Heathcliff also returns as a stranger following his mysterious absence, and finally, Linton Heathcliff arrives to disrupt his mother's family at the Grange and, subsequently, his father's 'family' at the Heights. This apparent paradox derives from the novel's exploration of the contemporary idea of the family. Although authorised and controlled by men, the nineteenth-century family is ideologically a feminine sphere; a private, inner space devoted to emotional and moral values, peace and harmony, and is hence liable to disruption by incursions from the ideologically masculine public world of struggle, acquisition, and competition.

The novel's geography might also be divided into separate spheres: the masculine world of hard work and the physical battle with nature at the Heights and the feminine world of luxury, leisure, culture, and the domestic ideal at the Grange. For the greater part of the novel, the Heights is presented as an actively masculine domain from which the feminine is progressively excluded. This process of exclusion begins with the death of Mrs Earnshaw and continues during Frances Earnshaw's brief sojourn at the Heights, where the feminine domain becomes confined to the parlour and Catherine is reconstructed to fit that newly restricted definition. Following Frances' death and Catherine's departure for the Grange, the Heights becomes an exclusively masculine domain, the site of physical aggression and violence. It also becomes the site of political aggression as Heathcliff seeks to acquire power over his former oppressors. In Isabella's account, in Chapter 17, the masculine violence at the Heights is so extreme as to become almost parodic. Isabella's catalogue of verbal abuse and physical violence concludes with this description of her own incorporation into the collective madness before her escape.

'[Heathcliff] snatched a dinner knife from the table and flung it at my head. It struck beneath my ear, and stopped the sentence I was uttering; but, pulling it out, I sprang to the door and delivered another which I hope went deeper than his missile.

'The last glimpse I caught of him was a furious rush on his part, checked by the embrace of his host; and both fell locked together on the hearth.

'In my flight through the kitchen . . . I knocked over Hareton, who was hanging a litter of puppies from a chair back in the doorway . . . ' (WH, 217)

Ironically, at the zenith of the Heights' barbarism Heathcliff prepares the way for its progressive recolonisation by the feminine, when he introduces Cathy as part of his schemes of revenge. The return of Nelly, who presides over Cathy's 'feminisation' of Hareton, completes the process. They establish their new order at the Heights while Heathcliff's aggressive energies and desire for power and dominance fade away. It is, however, symptomatic of this novel's refusal to resolve its contradictions that it resists being read as a simple myth of restoration and renewal. Although recolonised, the Heights is abandoned in favour of the Grange, and is left to the spirits of Catherine and Heathcliff, and the care of the misanthropic Joseph. The Heights, though abandoned, is not eradicated.

Heathcliff

For many readers Heathcliff is not only the central male character but also one of the central challenges of this novel. He is the man with no name, the stranger, who is in some ways less a character than a question or series of questions.

'Is Mr. Heathcliff a man? If so, is he mad? And if not, is he a devil?' (WH, 173)

'Is he a ghoul, or a vampire?' (WH, 359)

Isabella's and Nelly's questions have been echoed by generations of readers and critics, many of whom have seen Heathcliff as the novel's central enigma and the key to its meaning. Graham Holderness offers the most succinct version of this point of view when he asserts,

> Heathcliff is really the central problem of *Wuthering Heights*: our valuation of him determines our sense of what the novel is about.[2]

Terry Eagleton illuminates the nature of the problem in his equally crisp assertion that,

> No mere critical hair-splitting can account for the protracted debate over whether Heathcliff is hero or demon. (Eagleton, 100)

In Eagleton's reading Heathcliff is the novel's dominant figure. Heathcliff is also at the centre of Arnold Kettle's account, which presents him as the legitimate rebel against a repressive social order, a 'moral force' who 'wins our sympathy [because] we know he is on the side of humanity',[3] and who retains that sympathy even at his worst because 'we recognize a rough moral justice in what he has done to his oppressors'. Similarly Eagleton sees Heathcliff as a protean figure who stands at the centre of the text and draws all its threads into his person. Heathcliff is at once hero and villain, the oppressed and the oppressor, who is simultaneously the bearer of the novel's progressive forces and the embodiment of its contradictions.

In fact the shifting complexities of Heathcliff's class positions almost defy description. He enters the yeoman-farmer Earnshaw family as a *déclassé* outsider. Old Mr Earnshaw's attempts to incorporate him into this particular social order are thwarted by Hindley's efforts to 'reduce him to his right place' (WH, 64) by withdrawing education, separating him

from Catherine, and making him live and work as a
servant. Heathcliff's repetition of this process in his
own degradation of Hareton makes explicit the systematic
brutality and oppression which is implicit in the prevailing
social order. During his disappearance from the Heights
Heathcliff mysteriously acquires both culture and capital,
and when he re-enters the Earnshaw and Linton families the
oppressed has become the oppressor. Heathcliff's dynastic
and property ambitions do not represent an attempt to
become absorbed into the dominant social class, nor do
they offer a threat to the existing social structure. He seeks
simply to occupy the place of the dominant social class, and
to change his own and his heir's position within the existing
system of power relations.

> 'I want the triumph of seeing *my* descendant fairly
> lord of their estates; my child hiring their children
> to till their fathers' lands for wages.' (WH, 243)

Heathcliff's demonic energy is not only associated with
social and economic aggression, but also persistently
threatens to disrupt the sexual, familial and cultural
order. Psychoanalytic critics tend to associate this disruptive energy with 'libidinal desire' (Leo Bersani), or
'libidinal drive' and 'phallic energy' (James Kavanagh).
Kavanagh, for example, sees Heathcliff's 'primitive sexual-
social energy' as unleashing an 'anarchy of desire', which
is the driving force of a narrative whose key events are:
Heathcliff's disruption of Earnshaw family stability, and
his 'seduction of the daughter' of the family; his disruption
of the Linton family, and his 'seduction' of both the wife
(Catherine) and daughter/sister (Isabella); his monomaniac
plans to acquire the lands and homes of both the Earnshaw
and Linton families, and his abduction of the Linton
daughter.

Heathcliff's threat to the institution of the family is

sometimes seen as a clash between raw natural forces and the cultural order of custom, tradition and form. However, this view of Heathcliff tends to over-simplify the character and the novel, both of which represent multiple contradictions rather than a dualistic struggle of clearly opposed forces. Moreover, although the novel persistently associates Heathcliff with the primitive forces of nature, it also focuses on the way in which he is produced by, and operates within, a specific social and cultural order.

Many of those critics who see Heathcliff as the embodiment of natural or primitive libidinal desire, as a pre-social being, or as a rebel against a decadent and repressive social order, also see him as the novel's sole representative of authenticity and essential humanity.[4] The usual, though by no means inevitable, consequence of this view is the marginalisation of almost every other character in the novel, particularly the two Catherines and Hareton. Eagleton, for example, gives a full and sympathetic account of Heathcliff's struggle with the culture which seeks to contain him, and whose contradictions he embodies, but he is relatively uninterested in the details of Catherine's predicament and what it signifies, particularly the problems of gender politics which it raises. In Eagleton's version Catherine is simply the refuser of the bounty of Heathcliff's proffered gift.

> What Heathcliff offers Cathy is a non- or pre-social relationship, as the only authentic form of living in a world of exploitation and inequality, a world where one must refuse to measure oneself by the criteria of the class-structure. (138)

In the sexual politics of this account Heathcliff is the bearer of meaning and value, while Catherine is the empty vessel which might be filled with the content of Heathcliff's moral and ideological message.

It is perhaps time to remove Heathcliff from his lonely

position as the centre of the novel's meaning and value. We need to move beyond viewing this character as the single embodiment of the novel's social and sexual contradictions, and to view him instead as part of a pattern of relationships which figure those contradictions: contradictions which derive not only from class relations but from the social construction of gender and gender relations in a class society. I have tried to make such a move in earlier chapters by focusing attention on the two Catherines and Nelly, on the significance of the novel's narrative patterns and its adaptations of different fictional genres. In particular I have tried to show how *Wuthering Heights* uses its female characters and its generational structure to investigate the contradictory and changing pressures which shape ideas of gender, determine forms of familial and social life, and delimit the horizons of the imaginable.

It is important to reinsert Heathcliff into this complex of fictional relations. It is also useful to see this towering character in the context of a spectrum of male characters, by means of which the novel investigates and explores the social and cultural production of various masculinities. At one end of the spectrum is the motherless Heathcliff, all libidinal desire and phallic energy, the social outsider who is happiest when roaming the moors and who acquires the refinements of the drawing room for purely strategic purposes. At the other end of the spectrum is his son, Linton, whose natural habitat is the drawing room. Brought up exclusively by his mother, Linton Heathcliff is a sickly, enervated youth, the hypersensitive product of an over-refined culture.

Hindley occupies a place at the Heathcliffian end of the spectrum and, like Heathcliff, is both aggressive and competitive, although insecurely so. It is interesting to note that Hindley, like Heathcliff, is only fitfully subject to feminine influences, and that his brief marriage, ostensibly his most social period during which he actively cultivates a genteel domestic existence, is also a period of fierce domestic tyranny which excludes and oppresses Heathcliff and Catherine. Joseph, a dour, ascetic, misogynist is also placed at the Heathcliffian end of the spectrum. He is particularly closely identified with the Heights as masculine domain, and it is significant that he is left as its sole curator at the end of the novel's action.

At the Linton end of the spectrum Edgar is placed next to his nephew as a 'feminised' male, and he shares something of his nephew's nervous emotionalism, peevishness, and passivity. Edgar is, however, a more complex creation than Linton, and it is facile to dismiss him, as many critics have, as a mere milksop who offers Catherine a hollow, sterile gentility in place of the socially subversive authenticity offered by Heathcliff. Edgar is the benevolent face of patriarchy, although the family over which he presides is no less repressive and controlling than the other families in the novel. Edgar is a passive patriarch who exercises power without responsibility. When his authority is challenged he withdraws: when Catherine challenges him over Heathcliff, he withdraws to the library; when Isabella goes away with Heathcliff, he simply relinquishes all responsibility for her. However, he is not entirely selfish, and he has, at least, the virtues of gentleness and tenderness, as is shown in his care of Catherine in the later stages of her illness, in his devotion to his daughter, and in Nelly's commendation of him as a kind master. Edgar's relative virtues are revealed in the novel's comparison of the way in which three of the male characters respond to 'widowhood': Hindley becomes a ferocious drunk who threatens to murder his servant, and who almost kills his own child; Heathcliff succumbs to an excess of passion before steeling himself to his grim, self-appointed task of avenging himself on Catherine's family; Edgar, on the other hand, becomes a devoted – if over-indulgent and over-protective – father, who retreats from society and social duty, relinquishing his office of magistrate for a life of seclusion in his library.

However, it is Hareton who perhaps occupies the most interesting position towards the centre of this spectrum of male characters. Although he is represented with less imaginative power than Heathcliff, Hareton nevertheless occupies a central position in the novel's investigation of the construction of gendered subjects. As with most of the other characters Emily Brontë focuses on the unique set of social and genetic determinants which produce and reproduce Hareton. He is the son of a frail and passive mother of unknown social origin, and a weak but aggressive father whose position in the social and familial hierarchy is persistently threatened. In addition to his natural parents Hareton is also given a range of surrogate parents, who attempt to shape him according to their own needs and desires. In a sense Hareton's upbringing becomes the focus for a battle between contesting masculine and feminine forces. First, Nelly vies with a progressively brutalised Hindley to bring Hareton up according to her perceptions of what is suitable for a child of his social position. Nelly's efforts are systematically undone by Heathcliff, who seeks to reproduce in Hareton his own degradation by Hindley. This attempted reduction of Hareton to a state of crude nature is assisted by Joseph, who also contests, but is unable to resist, Hareton's final reconstruction under the feminine influence of Cathy and Nelly.

If we see Hareton as occupying the central position in the novel's spectrum of masculinities, and if in addition we see his character as the site of a struggle between contending masculine and feminine forces, we begin to move beyond the common view of Hareton as Heathcliff's textual shadow and surrogate, a pale imitation of Heathcliff who lacks his libidinal energy and socially subversive insurgence. Heathcliff claims Hareton as 'a personification of my youth . . . the ghost of my immortal love, my wild endeavour to hold my right, my degradation, my pride, my happiness, and my anguish' (WH, 353–4). But the novel as a whole offers a view of Hareton as the ghost revivified. The Hareton of the novel's concluding section is not a Heathcliff emasculated, but a Heathcliff socialised and feminised, and hence a Heathcliff whose energies become enabling and operative, rather than repressive and restrictive.

In its male characters, as well as in other aspects of its characterisation and structure, *Wuthering Heights* experimentally separates out and puts into opposition the realms of culture and nature, the socially constructed categories of the masculine and the feminine – and the men and women who inhabit them – and libidinal desire and socialised sexuality. Ultimately, in the figure of Hareton and in his relationship with Cathy, the novel provides a new fusion which partially resolves these oppositions, but it does so only by moving beyond prevailing social norms. As the novel approaches its incomplete closure, the masculine and feminine domains are fused, and nature (whose brutal potentialities have been exposed in the course of the narrative) is accommodated within a feminised culture. However, although socialised, the energies dramatised and explored in the novel do not become fully social. Although Hareton and Cathy establish a relationship of model mutuality which displaces the versions of the patriarchal family found in the first generation story, they will form their household away from the Heights, and indeed removed from the wider social world, in the private domestic enclosure of the Grange.

Wuthering Heights thus moves towards a workable centre, but it does not erase all its other elements in the process. While Heathcliff is not the single key which will unlock the novel's meanings, he nevertheless remains as a crucial strand in its network of relationships. On one level, as Miriam Allott has suggested, *Wuthering Heights* rejects Heathcliff,[5] and Hareton is one of the vehicles of his displacement. However, although he is displaced, Heathcliff is not expelled from the text. In Heathcliff's powerful fictional presence, and his persistence in the narrative in spirit form, the novel acknowledges both the force of libidinal desire and its continuing and inevitable challenge to the necessary repressions of civilisation. The profoundly ideological nature of its own narrative resolutions, the contradictions embodied and explored in the figure of Heathcliff, as in many other aspects of this complex novel, remain to trouble the momentary equilibrium of narrative closure.

9 Reading Women's Writing: Emily Brontë and the Critics

In *Literary Women* (1977), one of the first feminist literary histories to emerge from the post-1960s women's movement, Ellen Moers notes, almost in an aside, that the tradition of women's writing that her book attempts to construct 'mattered hardly at all' (43) in the case of Emily Brontë, who, unlike Jane Austen, for example, did not self-consciously write within, or seek support from, a tradition of women's literature. Throughout this study I have tried to show that there are a number of ways in which Emily Brontë's relationship to various traditions and views of women's writing matters a great deal. I have stressed the importance of *Wuthering Heights'* relationship to Female Gothic, and to the emerging realist Domestic novel, a genre widely used and read by women. I have also tried to suggest something of Brontë's relationship to, and reaction against, feminine traditions of nature and devotional poetry. In addition I have tried to show that her complex and problematic relationship, as a woman writer, to dominant masculine traditions and definitions of literature, or of particular literary genres, are also matters of great importance.

However, whatever importance we attach to the function of Emily Brontë's gender and her relation to female traditions as far as the production of her writing is concerned, it is clear that ideas about women's writing and its place in (or out) of the literary tradition have played a very important part in the ways in which her writings have been read.

The first readers of *Wuthering Heights* assumed, from the pseudonym, and on the evidence of the text, that its author was a man. Indeed G.W. Peck, in the *American Review* attributed both the novel's faults and virtues to the particular masculinity he constructs for its author. The novel's 'roughness' and 'savagery' is, simultaneously, the consequence of its author's coarse vulgarity and lack of familiarity with the 'society of gentlemen' (CH, 236), and of his laudable freedom from hypocrisy. Many other early reviewers found the novel 'coarse and disagreeable' (*Spectator*, CH, 217) and 'wildly grotesque' (*Britannia*, CH, 224), and professed themselves puzzled about its moral import. The *Examiner* was not alone in its failure to 'perceive any obvious moral in the story' (CH, 221). However, despite its capacity to shock, sicken and disgust, *Wuthering Heights* was also held to be 'puzzling', 'interesting' and 'remarkable' (*Jerrold's Weekly*, CH, 228). Many reviewers were struck by its originality and power, and some were inclined to think its author a young man of real promise.

Two of the reviews of the novel's first edition throw interesting light on some contemporary views of male and female writing, writers, and readers. The *Examiner*, for example, reveals misgivings about the feminisation of the novel, and articulates an implied theory of sexual difference in writing, according to which women's writing is coy, affected, and trivial, and men's writing is fearless, forthright, and probing.

We detest the affectation and *effeminate* frippery which is but too frequent in the modern novel, and willingly trust ourselves with an author who goes at once fearlessly into the moors and desolate places for his heroes; but we must at the same time stipulate with him that he shall

not drag into light all that he shall discover, of coarse and
loathsome, in his wanderings. (CH, 222, my emphasis)

The nature of the restrictions imposed on the male
writer's frankness by the existence of a largely female
novel-reading public is suggested by G.W. Peck's rather
paradoxical formulation of the double-think of the double
standard.

> If we did not know that this book had been read by
> thousands of young ladies in the country, we should
> esteem it our first duty to caution them against it simply
> on account of the coarseness of the style. (CH, 236)

As soon as the identities of the Brontë sisters were
revealed, their works became subject to the critical double
standard, the practice which judged women's writing by
different criteria from those applied to writing in general
(i.e. by men). Reviews of the second edition of *Wuthering
Heights* focused on issues of gender. The *Eclectic Review*,
for example, read the Brontës' novels through a theory of
gendered forms of writing in which women's writing is
tender and prone to exaggeration, while the writing of men
is bold, original, and subversive of convention. '[T]heir
instinctive attachments and occasional exaggerations, the
depths of their tenderness and their want of practical
judgement, all betoken the authorship of a lady' (CH,
297), but their works also have 'a certain masculine air'
revealed in 'a repudiation of conventionalisms and a bold
nervous cast of thought and action' (CH, 296).

When *Wuthering Heights* had been presumed to be
the work of a male author the *Athenaeum* had found it
powerful and clever, if somewhat gloomy and disagreeable.
The review of the 1850 edition, however, immediately
incorporated the Brontës into a tradition of peculiarly
English 'female genius', and *Wuthering Heights* became a

'more than usually interesting contribution to the history of female authorship in England' (CH, 295). Clearly, however, *Wuthering Heights* resisted easy appropriation into the nineteenth-century conception of a comfortable and marginalised tradition of female authorship. George Henry Lewes was not the only reviewer to find it 'curious enough . . . to read *Wuthering Heights* and *The Tenant of Wildfell Hall*, and remember that the writers were two retiring, solitary, consumptive girls' (*Leader*, CH, 292).

The difficulty posed by this 'curious' conjunction of powerful, imaginative fictions, 'coarse even for men' (CH, 292), with the fact of their female authorship continued to trouble critics throughout the nineteenth century. Some writers attempted to resolve the difficulty by holding firmly to their view of a separate and limited sphere of women's writing, and emphasised Emily Brontë's oddity and eccentricity in deviating from the implied norm. Thus, for W.C. Roscoe, she is a 'free undaunted spirit' (*National Review*, CH, 351) but a strange, distorted personality (see CH, 348), while the *Christian Remembrance* found her 'leanings and affinities were all of a weird character' (CH, 366).

Others attempted to relate Brontë's work to a newly emerging kind of woman and women's writing. D.G. Rossetti recommended *Wuthering Heights* as 'a fiend of a book . . . combining all the stronger female tendencies from Mrs. Browning to Mrs. Brownrigg [a midwife hanged for murder]' (CH, 300). Margaret Oliphant, on the other hand, saw the Brontë sisters as the reprehensible vanguard of a 'new generation' which disturbed the halcyon days of 'an orthodox system of novel making' by its 'wild declaration of the "Rights of Woman" in a new aspect' (CH, 311–2).

Later in the century a third response to Emily Brontë's challenging of the limiting definitions of 'the tradition of female authorship' led to her restoration to 'the rich main soil of English life and letters' (Mary Ward, CH, 452).

In two interesting examples of women reading women's writing, Mary Robinson and Mary Ward undertook a sympathetic re-examination of the particularities of Emily Brontë's works which attempted to locate them in the circumstances of her life, and in the broader context of the mainstream of English and European writing of the nineteenth century. Mary Robinson related *Wuthering Heights'* outspokenness, imaginative power, and unconventionality to the particular circumstances of its author's experience as a woman living and writing in a remote corner of the north of England. She emphatically resists Charlotte Brontë's apologetic tone and asserts that it was not the author's 'lack of knowledge of the world' that produced *Wuthering Heights*, 'not her inexperience, but rather her experience, limited and perverse . . . yet close and very real' (CH, 433). Mary Ward's attempt to place Emily Brontë's work within the mainstream of nineteenth-century writing lead to an even more fundamental reassessment than Robinson's. For Ward, Brontë's wildness, love of violence and exaltation of the self are precisely *not* merely the aberrations of a wild untutored female genius, but rather they belong 'to a particular European moment' of late Romanticism in which Emily Brontë's work 'holds a typical and representative place' (CH, 455).

Wuthering Heights generated far more attention and discussion in the nineteenth century than did the poems. Most early reviewers broadly accepted Charlotte Brontë's judgement of her sister's poetry. Mary Robinson, writing in 1883, is typical: 'The poems with their surplus of imagination, their instinctive music and irregular rightness of form, their sweeping impressiveness . . . are, indeed, not at all like the poetry women generally write' (CH, 431). For the most part, until quite recently, twentieth-century critics have continued to stress the individuality and eccentricity of Emily Brontë's poems; they are unusual, interesting, touched with lyric grace, but essentially they are minor off- shoots from the central poetic tradition. Since the 1970s, however, a developing feminist theory and criticism of poetry has provided us with new perspectives within which to view Emily Brontë's poems. Some feminist critics have attempted to insert the poems into their own construction of a 'distinctively female tradition' (Gilbert and Gubar (b), xxiv), but perhaps the most significant re-reading has come from the attempts by writers such as Cora Kaplan, Margaret Homans and Jan Montefiore (among others)[1] to explore the complex relations of the woman poet to the dominant traditions of poetry. Homans, in particular, has radically revised our view of Brontë's poems by reading them in the context of the problems posed for the woman poet by nineteenth-century Romantic definitions of poetry.

In the twentieth century *Wuthering Heights* has both acquired classic status and reached a wider popular audience. It has been dramatised, filmed, adapted for television, as well as read and studied on examination courses. As the novel became a classic, the question of its author's gender, which had played such an important part in contemporary controversies, receded into the background; once admitted into the canon of great writers, the author of *Wuthering Heights* became androgynous or genderless.

The question of Emily Brontë's gender having been, in a sense, erased by the acknowledgement of her greatness, the critics concentrated their attentions on the novel's form and its metaphysics. Its inclusion in the series of *Scrutiny* essays on 'The Novel as Dramatic Poem' (D.G. Klingopulos, 1947) neatly encapsulates a major focus of *Wuthering Heights* criticism down to the 1950s. In fact this shift of attention dates from Swinburne's essay of 1883, which compares the 'essentially tragic' genius of Brontë's 'poem' with that of the Elizabethan dramatists (CH, 440). A different kind of attentiveness to form was initiated by C.P. Sanger's *The Structure of 'Wuthering Heights'* (1926), a close structural analysis which demonstrated that, far from being clumsy and inartistic, Emily Brontë's novel was extremely carefully crafted and constructed, particularly in matters of chronology.

David Cecil also emphasised Brontë's structural skills in the essay in his *Early Victorian Novelists* (1934), widely regarded as the beginning of the novel's modern critical history. Cecil attempted a coherent synthesis of the novel's total meaning, which he saw as primarily religious, a dramatisation of the eternal and universal principles of storm and calm. Cecil has his own rather interesting answer to the problem of Emily Brontë's relationship to the dominant nineteenth-century literary tradition; he isolates her from her urbanised contemporaries, by virtue of what he takes to be her emphasis on man's relationship to the cosmos, rather than on social and psychological relations, and by allying her with a universal primitive Englishness, 'violent, unselfconscious, spiritual', redolent of the 'northern soil' (Cecil, 148). Cecil's metaphysical interpretation is echoed by Derek Traversi's '*Wuthering Heights* After a Hundred Years' (*Dublin Review*, 1949), which sees the novel as a work of 'pagan inspiration', and in J. Hillis Miller's *The Disappearance of God* (1963), which also considers the novel's central conception to be religious.

The emphasis on the novel's metaphysics more or less entirely displaced questions of gender. The author's gender was also a matter of no interest to the New Critics of the 1950s, who eschewed biographical and historical specificities in favour of an exclusive interest in the novel as verbal structure. During this period the novel's structure, imagery and narrative method all received exhaustive attention, as for example in Dorothy Van Ghent's much anthologised chapter from *The English Novel Form and Function* (1953).

In the past twenty years a burgeoning academic criticism has exhaustively explicated Emily Brontë's text. The

interest in myth, religion, and metaphysics has been
replaced by psychoanalytic studies and investigations of
the novel's representation of sexuality, such as Thomas
Moser's Freudian reading of the novel's recurrent sexual
symbolism,[2] and Leo Bersani's study of its version of the
Freudian 'family romance' (*A Future for Astyanax*, 1978).
Analysts of form have turned their attention to narrative
structure, and the novel's various levels of narrative and
narration.[3] There has also been some shifting of attention
from the central protagonists to the narrators and the
servants, and from Heathcliff to the two Catherines.

Many new perspectives have resulted from renewed
efforts to understand this extraordinary novel in relation to
the literary and historical situation in which it was written.
Robert Kiely, for example, locates it in the powerful
'counter-tradition' of nineteenth-century Romantic fiction.
For Kiely *Wuthering Heights*' status as the 'masterpiece'
of English Romantic fiction derives from exactly those
paradoxes and contradictions, and the mixing of styles and
modes, which some critics have interpreted as confusion
and lack of artistry. Where others see confusion, Kiely
sees multiplicity and complexity. '*Wuthering Heights* is like
dream *and* like life *and* like history *and* like other works of
literature precisely because Brontë rejects the exclusiveness
of these categories' (Kiely, 236).

Q.D. Leavis, on the other hand, acknowledges the power
of its Romantic affinities, but seeks to place the novel firmly
in the realist tradition. Leavis does indeed give the 'Fresh
Approach' promised by the title of her influential essay, and
despite the problematic nature of some of her assumptions
this remains one of the most sensible and thought-provoking
reassessments of the novel in the last twenty years. Leavis
values the novel for its 'truly human centrality' (137), and
concentrates on the complexity of its form and vision, and
the technical skills with which it conveys its 'human truths'
(138). She is particularly concerned with the way Brontë

gives a 'specific and informed sociological content' (98) to the Romantic writers' image of childhood in conflict with society. She is also very interested in the novel's representation of, and engagement with, a specific historical moment,

> when the old rough farming culture based on a *naturally* patriarchal family life, was to be challenged, tamed and routed by social and cultural changes that were to produce the Victorian class consciousness and the "unnatural" ideal of gentility. (99, my emphasis)

Leavis's essay also makes a decided and significant readjustment of the novel's centre of interest from Heathcliff to the two Catherines and Ellen Dean. Like Miriam Allott (*Essays in Criticism*, 8, 1958), although for different reasons, Leavis rejects Heathcliff. In her reading he 'is an enigmatic figure only by reason of his creator's indecision', he is 'an unsatisfactory composite with empty places in his history and no continuity of character' (96). Her case for the displacement of Heathcliff is perhaps damaged by overstatement, and Peter Widdowson speaks for the many readers who have responded positively to Heathcliff's power with his counter-assertion that 'Heathcliff is the centre and raison d'être of *Wuthering Heights*'.[4] Widdowson's own position is closer to those masculinist political readings which see Heathcliff as the supreme Romantic individual, whose single-minded passion for Catherine is an expression of an absolute integrity of self.

While it is not explicitly feminist, Leavis's reading of the novel is firmly woman-centred. The novel is the buried history of Catherine Earnshaw, her daughter, and Ellen Dean. Thus, Catherine Earnshaw is 'the real moral centre of the first half of the novel' (103), whose 'case' focuses on the nature and possibilities of womanhood and offers 'a method of discussing what being a woman means'. The limitations of Leavis's own view of womanhood are most evident in her study of Nelly, a vindication of this much-maligned character which relies on essentialist concepts of 'the *normal* woman, whose *truly feminine* nature' is revealed in 'spontaneous maternal impulses' (93, my emphases).

The most problematic aspect of Q.D. Leavis's reading (as with many others) is its attempt to grapple with the problem of producing a single coherent meaning for a text which seems to be characterised by openness, paradox, complexity, and indeterminacy. Her jettisoning of Heathcliff is merely one example of her stripping away of those 'recalcitrant elements' which obscure the 'truly creative' achievements of Emily Brontë's 'deeper intentions' (86–7). Frank Kermode,[5] using the perspectives of critical theorists such as Roland Barthes, has ably demonstrated the limitations of this monolithic method of reading.

Others have attempted to resolve or explore the novel's complexities by a more thoroughly historical analysis of its literary and social relations. The most influential of the socio-historical accounts are perhaps Arnold Kettle's *An Introduction to the English Novel*, Vol. 1 (1952) and Terry Eagleton's *Myths Of Power* (1975). Kettle presents Brontë as an uncompromising unromantic realist whose novel examines social change and challenges the complacent class attitudes of a middle-class readership. Terry Eagleton, on the other hand, is concerned with the novel's 'inner ideological structure', which he sees as a fictional representation of the contemporary historical struggle between the industrial bourgeoisie and the landed interest of the gentry and aristocracy. Where others see complexity, contradiction and paradox, Eagleton's Marxist account sees a dialectical confrontation of the 'tragic truth that the passion and society [the novel] presents are not fundamentally reconcilable' (100). Heathcliff, as the representative of an oppressed and/or insurgent proletariat, is the main focus of these readings, both of which are more

READING WOMEN'S WRITING   131

concerned with economic history than the history of gender, and with issues of class rather than sexual politics.

Feminist, or woman-centred critics have also played a major part in investigating *Wuthering Heights*' literary, social, and historical relations. Inga-Stina Ewbank's *Their Proper Sphere* (1966) was the first full-length study of the Brontë's '*as* early Victorian *Female* Novelists' (my emphases). Ewbank's fascinating account uses material from conduct books and periodicals to explore nineteenth-century ideas about women and their social and familial roles, and the ways in which these ideas affected contemporary women's writing. She attempts to show how Emily Brontë was, on the one hand, constrained by the limiting doctrine of the separate spheres and, on the other, empowered by her resistance to the prevailing restrictive definitions of women's writing.

The complex relations of the woman writer to the dominant, patriarchal literary tradition has exercised a number of writers since 1960s feminism began to make its impact on literary history and criticism. Ellen Moers (*Literary Women*, 1977) and Elaine Showalter (*A Literature of Their Own*, 1977), for example, seek to trace a specifically female literary tradition; not the marginalised 'separate sphere' of the nineteenth century, but one which is 'autonomous and self-defining, and purposefully and collectively concerns itself with the articulation of women's experience' (Showalter, 4). Both Moers and Showalter include Brontë in an active and oppositional sub-culture of women's writing which is oppressed by, but also resists, the limitations of the patriarchal tradition.

One of the most influential works from this phase of feminist criticism, at least among academic readers, was Sandra Gilbert and Susan Gubar's *The Madwoman in the Attic* (1979), which emphasises the psychic disablement of women writers by the tyrannical constraints of patriarchal writing. Gilbert and Gubar have been greatly influenced by

Harold Bloom's [6] work on the effects on later writers of 'the anxiety of influence' exerted by their literary predecessors. Their argument implies that the troubled relations between sons and their literary fathers are as nothing compared with the super-anxieties of writing daughters who, in Gilbert and Gubar's account, endlessly revise the writings of the literary patriarchs, subverting them by covert resistance and concealed or unconscious anger. In their version Emily Brontë is a writer more than usually haunted by 'Milton's bogey' (the phrase is Virginia Woolf's), and *Wuthering Heights* is a radical revision, even reversal, of Milton's misogynistic myth of the Fall, by way of Blake's rethinking of the relations between Heaven and Hell. By 'looking oppositely', they argue, Brontë not only found her own definitions of Heaven and Hell, but also sought her own female origins.

A very different view of the author emerges from Stevie Davies's portrait of *Emily Brontë: The Artist as a Free Woman* (1983). Davies's Brontë was not beset by the anxieties of the influence of patriarchal writing, but instead created Gondal as 'a place of female power where patriarchy (despite frequent incarceration of princesses) was not admired' (35). Davies radically changes the terms of the traditional debate about *Wuthering Heights* – often quite literally by simply substituting the term 'woman' for 'man'. Thus, she revises the long-held view that the novel is 'about' man's place in the cosmos, by declaring that it is 'about humanity in the person of the female' (105); the novel is not a myth of the fall, but 'a female vision of genesis, expulsion and rebirth'. In this reading the text, like Davies's version of Brontë, is androgynous: it is concerned with 'those aspects of human nature which cross the border of gender' (137), and with images of 'femininity' and 'masculinity' which are not unproblematically associated with the biologically female and male.

Davies's perspective in the early 1980s reflects a shift within feminism from an emphasis on woman's oppression to a concern with woman's power and ability. Reading from this perspective Carol Senf has claimed *Wuthering Heights* as 'Emily Brontë's version of Feminist History' (*Essays in Literature*, 12, 1985). Like Q.D. Leavis Senf foregrounds the 'buried story' of Catherine Earnshaw and her daughter, and shows how the novel exploits traditional genres and the structure of the family chronicle novel to produce an evolutionary feminised version of history in which women escape the tyranny of patriarchal history.

More recently, feminist critics, particularly Marxists, have sought to examine the functions of women's writing *within* patriarchy. Nancy Armstrong, for example, has examined how women writers are not only complicit in their own subjection (that is to say they implicitly and tacitly co-operate in their own oppression), but also help to perpetuate patriarchy by the way they have plotted the maps of their readers' imaginative world. Armstrong is particularly interested in *Wuthering Heights*' role in the development of a novelistic culture whose emphasis on the emotional and psychological life relegates politics to the margins of experience. Armstrong's writings are difficult, tendentious and overstated, but they offer a stimulating thinking-through of *Wuthering Heights*' historical relations, and the connections that it makes, or implies, between gender, class, culture, literature, society and politics.

Armstrong's work is profoundly influenced by Michel Foucault, the French cultural theorist and historian of sexuality, and by the work of the American Marxist Frederic Jameson on the 'political unconscious'. The psychoanalytic theories of Jacques Lacan underlie James Kavanagh's attempt to reread Emily Brontë in the late 1980s. Although Kavanagh's self-conscious attempt to read *Wuthering Heights* in the light of recent critical and psychoanalytic theories all too often reduces the novel to the parameters of those theories, nevertheless he does help to stimulate fresh thought about the novel.

Perhaps the most remarkable aspect of Kavanagh's book is its claim to resolve the 140 years of debate which I have summarised (and considerably truncated) in this chapter. The whole 'point' of *Wuthering Heights* is revealed at last. The 'point', we are told,

> is not to reveal the metaphysics of the elements, but to work out the structural possibilities for a family which is revolutionized as a socio-ideological institution by the pressures of insurgent capital, even as its psycho-sexual subjects are rent by the pressures of phallic desire (98).

Notwithstanding Kavanagh's confident assertion, most readers will continue to be puzzled and fascinated by a novel whose 'point' they find more resistant to discovery.

Feminist criticism, as I hope that this chapter and indeed the rest of this book have demonstrated, clarifies some of the complexities and difficulties of Emily Brontë's novel and poems. However, it also, inevitably, creates other difficulties, as it generates contradictory and conflicting meanings and views. As we explore and contest the meanings of Emily Brontë's writings in and for the late twentieth century, polemic and debate are just as important as they were when those writings were first read.

Notes

Note on Texts

(CH)   *The Brontës: The Critical Heritage*, ed. Miriam Allott (London, Routledge and Kegan Paul, 1974)

(H)   *The Complete Poems of Emily Jane Brontë*, ed. C.W. Hatfield (New York, Columbia University Press, 1941)

(LL)   *The Brontës: Their Lives, Friendships and Correspondence*, ed T.J. Wise and J.A. Symington (Oxford, Basil Blackwell, 1933), 4 vols

(WH)   *Wuthering Heights*, ed. David Daiches (Harmondsworth, Penguin, 1967).

In order to keep footnotes to the minimum I have usually footnoted only the first reference to a particular work. Subsequent references are given in the text.

Notes to Chapter 1

1. Edward Chitham, *A Life of Emily Brontë* (Oxford, Basil Blackwell, 1987).

2. John Hewish, *Emily Brontë: A Critical and Biographical Study* (London, Macmillan, 1969), p. 9.

3. Eva Figes, *Sex and Subterfuge: Women Novelists to 1850* (London, Macmillan, 1982), p. 26.

4. T.J. Wise and J.A. Symington (eds), *The Miscellaneous and Unpublished Writings of Charlotte and Patrick Branwell Brontë* (Oxford, Shakespeare Head, 1934), vol. 1, p. 1.

5. Elaine Showalter, *A Literature of Their Own: British Women Novelists from Brontë to Lessing* (London, Virago, 1979), p. 19.

6. George Henry Lewes, *The Leader*, 1 (May 18, 1850), p. 189.

7. George Eliot, 'Silly Novels by Lady Novelists', in *Essays of George Eliot*, ed. Thomas Pinney (London, Routledge and Kegan Paul, 1963), p. 304.

Notes to Chapter 2

1. Margaret Homans, *Women Writers and Poetic Identity: Dorothy Wordsworth, Emily Brontë and Emily Dickinson* (Princeton, N.J., Princeton University Press, 1980), p. 12.

2. Rosalind Miles, 'A Baby God: The Creative Dynamism of Emily

Brontë's Poetry', in *The Art of Emily Brontë*, ed. Anne Smith (London, Vision Press, 1976).

3. From the journal of the nineteenth-century American feminist, Margaret Fuller. Quoted in Sandra Gilbert and Susan Gubar, *The Madwoman in the Attic: the Woman Writer and the Nineteenth-Century Literary Imagination* (New Haven, Yale University Press, 1979), p. 69.

4. Cecil Day Lewis, 'The Poetry of Emily Brontë', *Brontë Society Transactions*, 67 (1957) pp. 83–9.

5. C.W. Hatfield, *The Complete Poems of Emily Jane Brontë* (New York, Columbia University Press, 1941 and 1967). References to this edition usually cite the number of the poem followed by a page reference.

6. Michael Wheeler, *English Fiction of the Victorian Period, 1830–1890* (London, Longman, 1985), p. 10.

7. Gilbert and Gubar, *The Madwoman in the Attic*. Subsequent references to this book are given in the text, citing Gilbert and Gubar (a).

8. Ellen Moers, *Literary Women* (London, Women's Press, 1978), p. 100.

9. Charlotte Brontë, *Jane Eyre*, World's Classics edn (Oxford, Oxford University Press, 1980), p. 86.

10. F.E. Ratchford, *Gondal's Queen* (Austin, University of Texas Press, 1955), p. 20.

11. Stevie Davies *Emily Brontë: the Artist as a Free Woman* (Manchester, Carcanet, 1983), p. 78.

12. Henry James, *Lectures on Literature* (London, Picador, 1983), p. 5.

13. Robin Gilmour, *The Novel in the Victorian Age: A Modern Introduction* (London, Edward Arnold, 1986), p. 10.

14. Michael Wheeler, op. cit., p. 67.

Notes to Chapter 3

1. Frederick G. Kenyon (ed.), *The Letters of Elizabeth Barrett Browning* (New York, Macmillan, 1897), vol. 1. pp. 230–232.

2. *Poems by Currer, Ellis and Acton Bell* (London, Aylott and Jones, 1846).

3. These lines are quoted in Leonore Davidoff and Catherine Hall, *Family Fortunes: Men and Women of the English Middle Classes 1780–1850* (London, Hutchinson, 1987), p. 343. The author was a reasonably well-to-do farmer's wife who ceased writing poetry from the birth of her first child, when she was 31, until the birth of her tenth and last child, when she was 44.

4. Cora Kaplan, *Salt and Bitter Good: Three Centuries of English and American Women Poets* (London, Paddington Press, 1975), p. 18.

5. John Hewish, op. cit., p. 17.

6. Louise Berkinow (ed.), *The World Split Open: Four Centuries of Women Poets in England and America* (New York, Random House, 1974), p. 26.

7. Muriel Spark and Derek Stanford, *Emily Brontë: Her Life and Work* (London, Peter Owen, 1960), p. 150.

8. F.E. Ratchford, op. cit., p. 12.

9. Nina Auerbach, 'This Changeful Life: Emily Brontë's Anti-Romance', in *Shakespeare's Sisters: Feminist Essays on Women Poets*, ed. by Sandra Gilbert and Susan Gubar (Bloomington, Indiana University Press, 1979), p. 49. Further references to this book are given in the text, citing Gilbert and Gubar (b).

10. George Eliot, *The Mill on the Floss* (Harmondsworth, Penguin, 1979), p. 381.

11. J. Hillis Miller, *The Disappearance of God* (Cambridge Mass., Harvard University Press, 1963), p. 160.

12. C. Day Lewis, op. cit., p. 97.

Notes to Chapter 4

1. Quoted in Patsy Stoneman, 'The Brontës and Death: Alternatives to Revolution', in *1848: The Sociology of Literature*, ed. Francis Barker *et al.* (Essex, University of Essex Press, 1978), p. 79.

2. This argument is developed in detail by Margaret Homans (op. cit.) to whom my own reading of Emily Brontë's poems is greatly indebted. See also Jan Montefiore, *Feminism and Poetry: Language, Experience, Identity in Women's Writing* (London, Pandora Press, 1987).

Notes to Chapter 5

1. Q.D. Leavis, 'A Fresh Approach to *Wuthering Heights*', in F.R. Leavis and Q.D. Leavis, *Lectures in America* (London, Chatto and Windus, 1969), p. 87.

2. Freud uses this term to describe the familial fantasies by means of which children attempt to resolve their confusions about identity and the boundaries of the self. Leo Bersani offers a sustained Freudian reading of *Wuthering Heights* in *A Future for Astyanax: Character and Desire in Literature* (London, Marion Boyars, 1978).

3. See Ellen Moers, and Eva Figes, op. cit. Also Tania Modleski, *Loving With a Vengeance: Mass Produced Fantasies for Women* (London, Methuen, 1984), and Jane Spencer, *The Rise of the Woman Novelist: From Aphra Behn to Jane Austen* (Oxford, Basil Blackwell, 1986).

4. N.M. Jacobs, 'Gendered and Layered Narrative in *Wuthering Heights* and *The Tenant of Wildfell Hall*', *Journal of Narrative Technique*, 16 (1986), p. 204.

5. Leo Bersani, op. cit., p. 221.

6. Rosemary Jackson, *Fantasy: The Literature of Subversion* (London, Methuen, 1981), p. 124.

7. Carol Senf, 'Emily Brontë's Version of Feminist History: *Wuthering Heights*', *Essays in Literature*, 12 (1985), p. 209.

8. Judith Lowder Newton, *Women, Power and Subversion: Social Strategies in British Fiction, 1778–1860* (London, Methuen, 1985), p. 13.

Notes to Chapter 6

1. Sigmund Freud, 'Femininity', from 'New Introductory Lectures on Psychoanalysis' in *The Standard Edition of the Complete Works of Sigmund Freud*, ed. James Strachey (New York, Norton, 1976), vol. XXII, p. 116.

2. Sarah Ellis, quoted in Judith Lowder Newton, op. cit., p. 5 and p. 1.

3. Terry Eagleton, *Myths of Power: A Marxist Study of the Brontës* (London, Macmillan, 1975), p. 118.

Notes to Chapter 7

1. Robert Kiely, *The Romantic Novel in England* (Cambridge, Mass., Harvard University Press, 1972), and N.M. Jacobs, op. cit.

2. James Kavanagh, *Emily Brontë* (Oxford, Basil Blackwell, 1985), p. 31.

3. Carol Senf, op. cit., p. 207.

Notes to Chapter 8

1. D.H. Lawrence, *The Rainbow* (Harmondsworth, Penguin, 1970), p. 11.

2. Graham Holderness, *Wuthering Heights* (Milton Keynes, Open University Press, 1985), p. 13.

3. Arnold Kettle, *Introduction to the English Novel* vol. I (London, Hutchinson, 1951), p. 135.

4. See Leo Bersani, Rosemary Jackson, and Arnold Kettle, op. cit.

5. Miriam Allott, 'The Rejection of Heathcliff?', *Essays in Criticism*, 8 (1958), p. 27.

Notes to Chapter 9

1. See notes to Chapters 3 and 4.

2. Thomas Moser, 'What is the Matter with Emily Jane? Conflicting Impulses in *Wuthering Heights*', Nineteenth Century Fiction, 17, (1962).

3. For example N.M. Jacobs, op. cit.

4. Peter Widdowson, 'Emily Brontë; the romantic novelist', *Moderne Sprachen*, 66 (1972).

5. See *The Classic: Literary Images of Permanence and Change* (Cambridge, Mass., Harvard University Press, 1983).

6. See, for example, *The Anxiety of Influence: A Theory of Poetry* (New York, Oxford University Press, 1973).

Bibliography

Selected Works by Emily Brontë

The Brontës: Their Lives, Friendships and Correspondence, eds T.J. Wise and J.A. Symington, 4 vols (Oxford, Shakespeare Head, 1933).
Poems by Currer, Ellis and Acton Bell (London, Aylott and Jones, 1846).
The Complete Poems of Emily Jane Brontë, ed. C.W. Hatfield (New York, Columbia University Press, 1941).
Wuthering Heights: A Novel, by Ellis Bell, with *Agnes Grey*, by Acton Bell, 3 vols (London, T.C. Newby, 1847).
Wuthering Heights, ed. and intro., David Daiches (Harmondsworth, Penguin, 1967).

Selected Works about Emily Brontë: including general works of feminist literary history

Allott, Miriam (ed.), *The Brontës: The Critical Heritage* (London, Routledge and Kegan Paul, 1974).
—— (ed.), *'Wuthering Heights': A Selection of Critical Essays* (London, Macmillan, 1970).
—— 'The Rejection of Heathcliff?', *Essays in Criticism*, 8 (1958), pp. 27–47.
Armstrong, Nancy, *Desire and Domestic fiction* (New York, Oxford University Press, 1987).
—— 'Emily Brontë in and out of her time', *Genre*, 15 (1982), pp. 243–64.
—— 'The Rise of Feminine Authority in the Novel', *Novel*, 15 (1982), pp. 127–45.
Basch, Francoise, *Relative Creatures: Victorian Women in Society and the Novel, 1837–67*, trans. Anthony Rudolf (London, Allen Lane, 1974).
Bersani, Leo, *A Future for Astyanax: Character and Desire in Literature* (London, Marion Boyars, 1978).
Cecil, David, *Early Victorian Novelists: Essays in Revaluation* (London, Constable, 1960).

Chitham, Edward, *A Life of Emily Brontë* (Oxford, Basil Blackwell, 1987).

—— *The Brontës' Irish Background* (London, Macmillan, 1986).

Christian, Mildred, 'The Brontës' in *Victorian Fiction: A Guide to Research*, ed. Lionel Stevenson (Cambridge, Mass., Harvard University Press, 1967).

Colby, Vineta, *The Singular Anomaly: Woman Novelists of the Nineteenth Century* (London, Athlone, 1970).

Craik, Wendy, *The Brontë Novels* (London, Methuen, 1968).

Davies, Stevie, *Emily Brontë: The Artist as a Free Woman* (Manchester, Carcanet, 1983).

Day-Lewis, Cecil, 'The Poetry of Emily Brontë', *Brontë Society Transactions* 67 (1957), pp. 83–99.

Eagleton, Terry, *Myths of Power: A Marxist Study of the Brontës* (London, Macmillan, 1975).

Ewbank, Inga-Stina, *Their Proper Sphere: A Study of the Brontë Sisters as Early Victorian Female Novelists* (London, Edward Arnold, 1966).

Figes, Eva, *Sex and Subterfuge: Women Novelists to 1850* (London, Macmillan, 1982).

Gaskell, Elizabeth, *The Life of Charlotte Brontë* (London, Dent, 1974).

Gérin, Winifred, *Emily Brontë: A Biography* (Oxford, Oxford University Press, 1972).

Ghent, Dorothy Van, *The English Novel Form and Function* (New York, Rinehart, 1953).

Gilbert, Sandra and Gubar, Susan, *The Madwoman in the Attic: The Woman Writer and the Nineteenth-Century Literary Imagination* (New Haven, Yale University Press, 1978).

—— (eds) *Shakespeare's Sisters: Feminist Essays on Women Poets* (Bloomington, Indiana University Press, 1979).

Gregor, Ian, *The Brontës: A Collection of Critical Essays* (Englewood Cliffs, Prentice Hall, 1970).

Hewish, John, *Emily Brontë: A Critical and Biographical Study* (London, Macmillan, 1969).

Homans, Margaret, *Women Writers and Poetic Identity: Dorothy Wordsworth, Emily Brontë and Emily Dickinson* (Princeton, Princeton University Press, 1980).

Jacobs, N.M., 'Gendered and Layered Narrative in *Wuthering Heights* and *The Tenant of Wildfell Hall*', *Journal of Narrative Technique*, 16 (1986), pp. 204–19.

Jackson, Rosemary, *Fantasy: The Literature of Subversion* (London, Methuen, 1981).

Kaplan, Cora, *Salt and Bitter Good: Three Centuries of English and American Women Poets* (London, Paddington Press, 1975).

Kiely, Robert, *The Romantic Novel in England* (Cambridge, Mass., Harvard University Press, 1972).

Klingopulos, D.G., 'The Novel as Dramatic Poem', *Scrutiny*, XIV (1947).

Leavis, Q.D.L., 'A Fresh Approach to *Wuthering Heights*' in F.R. Leavis and Q.D. Leavis, *Lectures in America* (London, Chatto and Windus, 1969).

Lovell, Terry, *Consuming Fiction* (London, Verso, 1987).

Miller, Jane, *Women Writing About Men* (London, Virago, 1986).

Moers, Ellen, *Literary Women* (London, Women's Press, 1978).

Montefiore, Jan, *Feminism and Poetry: Language, Experience, Identity in Women's Writing* (London, Pandora Press, 1987).

Moser, Thomas, 'What is the matter with Emily Jane? Conflicting impulses in *Wuthering Heights*', *Nineteenth Century Fiction*, 17 (1962), pp. 1–19.

Newton, Judith, Lowder, *Woman Power and Subversion: Social Strategies in British Fiction 1778–1860* (London, Methuen, 1985).

—— and Rosenfelt, Deborah (eds), *Feminist Criticism and Social Change: Sex, Class and Race in Literature and Culture* (London, Methuen, 1985).

Ohman, Carol, 'Emily Brontë in the Hands of Male Critics', *College English*, 32 (1971), pp. 706–13.

Ratchford, F.E., *The Brontës' Web of Childhood* (New York, Columbia University Press, 1941).

—— *Gondal's Queen* (Austin, University of Texas Press, 1955).

Rich, Adrienne, *On Lies, Secrets and Silence: Selected Prose 1966–1978* (London, Virago, 1980).

Rosengarten, Herbert J., 'The Brontës' in *Victorian Fiction: A Second Guide to Research*, ed. George H. Ford (Cambridge, Mass., Harvard University Press, 1978).

Sanger, C.P., 'The Structure of *Wuthering Heights*', *Hogarth Essays*, 19 (1926), pp. 193–208. Reprinted in the Allott and Gregor collections.

Showalter, Elaine, *A Literature of Their Own: Women Novelists from Brontë to Lessing* (London, Virago, 1979).

—— (ed.), *The New Feminist Criticism: Essays on women, literature, and theory* (London, Virago, 1986).

Smith, Anne (ed.), *The Art of Emily Brontë* (London, Vision Press, 1976).

Thompson, Patricia, *The Victorian Heroine: A Changing Ideal* (Oxford University Press, 1956).

Tillotson, Kathleen, *Novels of the Eighteen-Forties* (Oxford, Oxford University Press, 1956).

Traversi, Derek, '*Wuthering Heights* After a Hundred Years', *Dublin Review*, 245 (1949).

Visick, Mary, *The Genesis of 'Wuthering Heights'* (1960; 3rd edition, London, Ian Hodgkins, 1980).

Winnifrith, Tom, *The Brontës and Their Background: Romance and Reality* (London, Macmillan, 1973).

Index